Privacy and the Internet:
Your Expectations and Rights Under the Law

Second Edition

Revised and Updated by

Margaret C. Jasper

Oceana's Legal Almanac Series:
Law for the Layperson

Oceana®

NEW YORK

OXFORD
UNIVERSITY PRESS

*Oxford University Press, Inc., publishes works that further Oxford University's
objective of excellence in research, scholarship, and education.*

Copyright © 2009 by Oxford University Press, Inc.
Published by Oxford University Press, Inc.
198 Madison Avenue, New York, New York 10016

Library of Congress Cataloging-in-Publication Data

Jasper, Margaret C.
Privacy and the Internet : your expectations and rights under
the law / by Margaret C. Jasper. — 2nd ed.
    p. cm. — (Oceana's legal almanac series. Law for the layperson,
ISSN 1075-7376)
Includes bibliographical references.
ISBN 978-0-19-537808-5 ((hardback) : alk. paper)
1. Data protection—Law and legislation—United States—Popular works.
2. Internet—Law and legislation—United States—Popular works. 3. Privacy, Right
of—United States—Popular works. I. Title.
KF1263.C65J38 2009
342.7308'58—dc22   2008053955

Note to Readers:
This publication is designed to provide accurate and authoritative information in regard to
the subject matter covered. It is based upon sources believed to be accurate and reliable and
is intended to be current as of the time it was written. It is sold with the understanding that
the publisher is not engaged in rendering legal, accounting, or other professional services. If
legal advice or other expert assistance is required, the services of a competent professional
person should be sought. Also, to confirm that the information has not been affected or
changed by recent developments, traditional legal research techniques should be used, including checking primary sources where appropriate.

*(Based on the Declaration of Principles jointly adopted by a Committee of the
American Bar Association and a Committee of Publishers and Associations.)*

You may order this or any other Oxford University Press publication
by visiting the Oxford University Press website at www.oup.com

To My Husband Chris

Your love and support

are my motivation and inspiration

To My Sons, Michael, Nick and Chris

-and-

In memory of my son, Jimmy

Table of Contents

CHAPTER 3:
E-COMMERCE

CHAPTER 4:
ONLINE FINANCIAL SERVICES

CHAPTER 5:
PROTECTING CHILDREN'S PRIVACY ONLINE

ABOUT THE AUTHOR

MARGARET C. JASPER is an attorney engaged in the general practice of law in South Salem, New York, concentrating in the areas of personal injury and entertainment law. Ms. Jasper holds a Juris Doctor degree from Pace University School of Law, White Plains, New York, is a member of the New York and Connecticut bars, and is certified to practice before the United States District Courts for the Southern and Eastern Districts of New York, the United States Court of Appeals for the Second Circuit, and the United States Supreme Court.

Ms. Jasper has been appointed to the law guardian panel for the Family Court of the State of New York, is a member of a number of professional organizations and associations, and is a New York State licensed real estate broker operating as Jasper Real Estate, in South Salem, New York.

Margaret Jasper maintains a website at http://www.JasperLawOffice.com.

In 2004, Ms. Jasper successfully argued a case before the New York Court of Appeals, which gives mothers of babies who are stillborn due to medical negligence the right to bring a legal action and recover emotional distress damages. This successful appeal overturned a 26-year old New York case precedent, which previously prevented mothers of stillborn babies from suing their negligent medical providers.

Ms. Jasper is the author and general editor of the following Legal Almanacs:

AIDS Law (3d Ed.)

The Americans with Disabilities Act (2d Ed.)

Animal Rights Law (2d Ed.)

Auto Leasing

Bankruptcy Law for the Individual Debtor

Banks and Their Customers (3d Ed.)

Becoming a Citizen

Buying and Selling Your Home

Commercial Law

Consumer Rights Law

Co-ops and Condominiums: Your Rights and Obligations as an Owner

Credit Cards and the Law (2d Ed.)

Custodial Rights

Dealing with Debt

Dictionary of Selected Legal Terms (2d Ed.)

Drunk Driving Law

DWI, DUI and the Law

Education Law

Elder Law (2d Ed.)

Employee Rights in the Workplace (2d Ed.)

Employment Discrimination Under Title VII (2d Ed.)

Environmental Law (2d Ed.)

Estate Planning

Everyday Legal Forms

Executors and Personal Representatives: Rights and Responsibilities

Guardianship, Conservatorship and the Law

Harassment in the Workplace

Health Care and Your Rights Under the Law

Health Care Directives

Hiring Household Help and Contractors: Your Obligations Under the Law

Home Mortgage Law Primer (3d Ed.)

Hospital Liability Law (2d Ed.)

How to Change Your Name

How to Form an LLC

How to Protect Your Challenged Child

How to Start Your Own Business

Identity Theft and How to Protect Yourself

Individual Bankruptcy and Restructuring (2d Ed.)

Injured on the Job: Employee Rights, Worker's Compensation and Disability

Insurance Law

International Adoption

Juvenile Justice and Children's Law (2d Ed.)

Labor Law (2d Ed.)

Landlord-Tenant Law

Law for the Small Business Owner (2d Ed.)

The Law of Adoption

The Law of Attachment and Garnishment (2d Ed.)

The Law of Buying and Selling (2d Ed.)

The Law of Capital Punishment (2d Ed.)

The Law of Child Custody

The Law of Contracts

The Law of Copyright (2d Ed.)

The Law of Debt Collection (2d Ed.)

The Law of Alternative Dispute Resolution (2d Ed.)

The Law of Immigration (2d Ed.)

The Law of Libel and Slander

The Law of Medical Malpractice (2d Ed.)

The Law of No-Fault Insurance (2d Ed.)

The Law of Obscenity and Pornography (2d Ed.)

The Law of Patents

The Law of Personal Injury (2d Ed.)

The Law of Premises Liability (2d Ed.)

The Law of Product Liability (2d Ed.)

The Law of Special Education (2d Ed.)

The Law of Speech and the First Amendment

The Law of Trademarks

The Law of Violence Against Women (2d Ed.)

Lemon Laws

Living Together: Practical Legal Issues

Marriage and Divorce (3d Ed.)

Missing and Exploited Children: How to Protect Your Child

More Everyday Legal Forms

Motor Vehicle and Traffic Law

Nursing Home Negligence

Pet Law

Prescription Drugs

Privacy and the Internet: Your Rights and Expectations Under the Law (2d Ed.)

Probate Law

Protecting Your Business: Disaster Preparation and the Law

Real Estate Law for the Homeowner and Broker (2d Ed.)

Religion and the Law

Retirement Planning

The Right to Die (2d Ed.)

Rights of Single Parents

Small Claims Court

Social Security Law (2d Ed.)

Teenagers and Substance Abuse

Transportation Law: Passenger Rights & Responsibilities

Trouble Next Door: What to Do with Your Neighbor

Veterans' Rights and Benefits

Victim's Rights Law

Welfare: Your Rights and the Law

What If It Happened to You: Violent Crimes and Victims' Rights

What If the Product Doesn't Work: Warranties & Guarantees

Workers' Compensation Law (2d Ed.)

Your Child's Legal Rights: An Overview

Your Rights in a Class Action Suit

Your Rights as a Tenant

Your Rights Under the Family and Medical Leave Act

You've Been Fired: Your Rights and Remedies

INTRODUCTION

The Internet has become a significant source of both commercial and financial activity, and has become this nation's primary medium for the exchange of news, mail, and general information. Unfortunately, these great benefits expose Internet users to serious privacy risks, which can lead to catastrophic results. Thus it is crucial that Internet users understand how to safely and securely "surf the net," without exposing themselves to all sorts of criminal activity and other intrusions into their personal information.

This Almanac discusses some of the most important security methods, including the effective use of passwords, utilizing virus software, installing firewalls, understanding encryption technology, and being vigilant about the type of information one shares on the Internet. The problem of Internet identity theft is also presented as an overview.

The legal obligations of various entities, particularly financial institutions, of protecting the private information of Internet users is also explored, including Internet privacy policies and applicable laws. A discussion of online privacy protection for children, which encompasses the governing law is included.

In addition, this Almanac sets forth the role of the Federal Trade Commission (FTC) in enforcing privacy rights, including a review of some of the major enforcement cases brought by the FTC.

The Appendix provides resource directories, applicable statutes, and other pertinent information and data. The Glossary contains definitions of many of the terms used throughout the Almanac.

CHAPTER 1:
SECURING YOUR COMPUTER

IN GENERAL

The "Internet" was initially conceived for military purposes in 1962 as a decentralized computer network to protect the ability of the military command to communicate in case of a nuclear attack. It took seven years to develop the prototype, which initially consisted of four computer networks located at three universities and one research facility.

Since that time, the Internet has grown tremendously. It has provided the public with a revolutionary tool for marketing, banking and communication. We are able to access all sorts of information and entertainment; perform banking and other financial activities online; purchase products from all over the world; and even work conveniently from home or away while still being able to communicate efficiently with our main office location.

Unfortunately, along with the tremendous advantages the Internet provides, there are great risks. Internet use opens up a gateway to our personal information, our security and safety. The Internet enhances the availability and accessibility of personal identifying information, and thus creates greater risks for consumers and greater opportunities for criminal activity.

Registering for online services generally requires the consumer to provide personal information, including financial information. In addition, there are many scams being perpetrated on the Internet that fool the consumer into revealing personal information. Those seeking to invade the privacy of Internet users, often for criminal purposes, are constantly seeking to decode the massive amount of data being transmitted on the Internet.

In addition, the Internet has become a popular social networking system for adults and children. There are chat rooms, online dating services, and virtual reality "cybersocieties" where individuals meet and socialize with each other in cyberspace. Unfortunately, there are predators who visit these websites with no good intentions. Thus it is important for all those who engage in social networking on the Internet to be aware of potential dangers. This is particularly important for children who are naïve and more likely to be lured into an unsafe and risky situation.

Therefore, it is crucial that Internet users carefully safeguard their personal information to protect their privacy and minimize the risk of becoming a victim. As further discussed in this Almanac, securing a computer and protecting one's personal information is largely a matter of routine maintenance. Nevertheless, these procedures are frequently neglected by the average Internet user, exposing them to a potential disaster.

When an individual signs on to the Internet though an Internet Service Provider (ISP), they engage in "online communication." The information that they communicate necessarily passes through multiple computer systems to reach its destination. As the information passes through the various computer systems, the capability of the computer system to "capture" and "store" the information exists.

There is no way that anyone using the Internet can be guaranteed complete privacy of the information transmitted online. Nevertheless, as discussed below, the degree to which one's personal information is potentially exposed depends, in large part, on the nature of their online activity.

INTERNET ACCESS

Dial-Up

Dial-up Internet access is achieved by using existing telephone lines. A modem is used to connect the telephone line to an Internet Service Provider (ISP) with whom the user has an account. In rural areas, dial-up service may be the only way to access the Internet. Unfortunately, dial-up service is slow and the quality of the connection is inferior. Internet pages load very slowly and it is difficult to stream media, such as audio and video content.

Broadband

Broadband Internet access—also known as "high speed" Internet access—has largely replaced dial-up service for most Internet users.

With broadband access, you do not have to "dial-up" to reach your Internet Service Provider, you simply turn on your computer.

Types of Broadband Service

Broadband Internet access available in most areas for residential service includes cable modem, digital subscriber line (DSL), fiber optic, and wireless.

Cable Modem

Cable modem Internet access is generally offered by the same company that provides the area's cable television service. Cable modems access the Internet over cable lines without interfering with cable television service.

Digital Subscriber Lines (DSL)

Digital Subscriber Lines (DSL) Internet access is generally offered by local telephone companies. DSL accesses the Internet through phone lines without interfering with telephone service.

Fiber Optic

Fiber optic Internet access is the newest technology, which provides faster service. Fiber optic lines provide access to the Internet, and can also provide telephone and television services. Fiber optic broadband service is not yet available in all areas.

Wireless

Wireless Internet access is available from cell phone providers. The Internet is accessed through wireless telephones and PDA devices.

Broadband Risk Factors

Broadband service keeps the consumer connected to the Internet whenever their computer is turned on as opposed to signing on and off each time they want to go online. However, this convenience has made broadband users more vulnerable to having their private information accessed than dial-up users. Thus you should consider installing a "firewall," i.e., special software that provides a barrier and controls access to a computer by unauthorized users.

Hackers are able to access computers through an open Internet connection giving them access to the user's private information. When the Internet connection is on all day and night, it is easier for hackers to break into your computer. To minimize the risk, it is important to log off the Internet after each session. Any computer connected to the Internet is a potential target for malicious hackers.

WIRELESS NETWORKS

Many computer users now access the Internet through wireless networks. It is convenient and allows you to work on a laptop anywhere, provided you are within the network's range. Wireless Internet access requires a broadband connection into your home, e.g., a cable modem or DSL, as described above. This is called the "access point." The access point is connected to a wireless router—a device that connects networks—which broadcasts a signal through the air.

Risk Factors and Security Measures

The wireless network presents certain risks because any computer that has a wireless card installed, and which is within range of your network, can "pull the signal" from the air and access the Internet. Therefore, another individual within range can use your network to access the Internet, and hackers can access the information on your computer.

Therefore, it is important to protect your wireless network by taking certain precautionary measures, as discussed below.

Encryption

Encryption is the best way to secure your wireless network. This technology scrambles data so that it is unreadable to unauthorized users. Most wireless routers have encryption software built into the device, however, it is usually turned off and must be turned on to activate the feature. There are two types of encryption: (1) Wi-Fi Protected Access (WPA); and (2) Wired Equivalent Privacy (WEP). Your computer and router must use the same encryption.

Firewall/Anti-Virus Software

You should install a firewall—software that acts as a barrier to unwanted and unauthorized access to your computer—as well as anti-virus and anti-spyware software, and keep them up-to-date.

Turn Off Identifier Broadcasting

Most wireless routers have a mechanism called identifier broadcasting that sends out a signal to any device in the vicinity announcing its presence. This is unnecessary and hackers can use identifier broadcasting to access vulnerable wireless networks. If your wireless router permits, you should turn off the identifier broadcasting mechanism.

In addition, you should change the identifier on your router from the default setting, which may be known to a hacker, to a unique identifier that only you know. When you change the identifier on the router, your computer must be set to the same identifier in order to communicate.

Administrative Password Protection

Change the wireless router's administrative password from the default password, which may be known to a hacker, to a unique password that is at least 10 characters long. The longer the password, the harder it is for a hacker to break the code.

Setting Your Media Access Control (MAC)

Every computer that is permitted to communicate with a wireless network is assigned its own unique Media Access Control (MAC) address. You should set the wireless router's mechanism so that it only allows computers with particular MAC addresses to access the network.

Turn Off Your Wireless Network

When you are not using your wireless network to access the Internet, you should turn it off. Hackers cannot access a wireless router when it is off.

Wi-Fi Hotspots

Many businesses open to the public—such as restaurants, coffee shops, hotels, and airports, etc.—provide Wi-Fi service—wireless Internet access—to attract customers. These are known as "Wi-Fi Hotspots." You cannot assume that these businesses offer secure connections.

Although convenient, Wi-Fi presents a number of security problems as it is relatively easy to hack into a wireless network even when wireless encryption standards have been configured. It is crucial that you employ effective security measures when using public wireless technology or risk unauthorized accidental or intentional access to their private data files.

This is particularly important for businesses that need to protect sensitive proprietary information and confidential files. A recent study of business centers in New York City, San Francisco, London and Frankfurt revealed that more than one-third of wireless business networks were found to be unsecured. Using a laptop computer, the researchers were able to access information from wireless business networks simply by driving around the city streets.

Therefore, you should be careful about the information you access or send from a public wireless network. To be on the safe side, you may want to assume that other people can access any information you see or send over a public wireless network. Unless you can verify that a hot spot has effective security measures in place, it may be best to avoid sending or receiving sensitive information over that network.

VOICE OVER INTERNET PROTOCOL (VoIP)

Voice over Internet Protocol (VoIP) is a technology that allows computer users to make and receive telephone calls using a broadband Internet connection instead of a regular telephone line. VoIP converts the voice signal from your phone call into a digital signal that travels through the Internet to the person you are calling. If you are calling a regular telephone number, the signal is converted back to voice on the receiving end. Generally, you can call any telephone number and receive calls from any telephone number.

VoIP technology is available through some telephone and cable companies, some Internet Service Providers, and companies that specialize in the service. However, before signing up for this new technology, you should be aware of some risk factors and find out what kind of security measures are available.

Because VoIP calls are transmitted over the Internet, this raises security concerns. For example, VoIP services can be attacked by computer viruses, and you may start receiving Spam over Internet Telephony (SPIT), a new kind of spam, that leaves a massive number of voice mail messages in your inbox.

BEWARE OF MALWARE

The term "malware" refers to malicious software, such as viruses and spyware, which has been illegally installed on your computer without your knowledge or consent. Malware is used to monitor or control your computer use. A hacker will use a number of tactics to try and trick you into installing malware on your computer, e.g., by posting interesting links and downloads. Once the malware is installed, the hacker is able to steal your personal information.

If you are constantly getting pop-up windows; strange icons or toolbars; error messages; keys that don't work properly; sluggish performance; or you are redirected to websites for no reason, these are all warnings signs that malware may have been installed on your computer.

To minimize the risk of malware infecting your computer, you should install a firewall, as well as anti-virus and anti-spyware software, and regularly update the software. Make sure your operating system and security software are updated automatically to provide the highest level of security. Make sure your browser security feature is set high enough to detect unauthorized downloads.

In addition, do not download software from unfamiliar websites or you risk infecting your computer with malware. The same rule applies to unfamiliar software. Close any pop-up windows by clicking on the X icon in the title bar. Do not click on any links in pop-up windows or spam e-mails as that may start an unauthorized download on your computer.

Malware can lead to identity theft, therefore, it is important to be able to recognize when malware has infected your computer so you can delete it before it causes you problems. If you believe that malware is on your computer, do not do any online banking or shopping until you have detected and deleted it from your computer.

You should file a complaint with your Internet Service Provider so that they are made aware of the malware threat. You should also file a complaint with the Federal Trade Commission (FTC).

FILE-SHARING RISKS

File-sharing is a popular online activity. People share music, software, and information through a P2P network. In order to share files, special software must be installed that connects your computer to other computers running the same software. There could be millions of users connected to the network simultaneously. The positive result of file-sharing is the enormous amount of information that can be obtained. Unfortunately, however, there are also privacy risks with file-sharing.

For example, when you are connected to the file-sharing network, you may inadvertently provide access to your private files that contain personal information. In addition, you may download a virus or spyware, as discussed above.

To minimize your privacy risks, you should be very careful when you install the file-sharing software. You must make sure that you do not make any changes to the software's default settings or you risk opening up your private folders to all other P2P users. In addition, by default, the file-sharing application will share any downloads that are stored in your download folder. If you do not want to share these files, you must make the correct settings when you install the software.

As discussed above, you should install a firewall and security software, and make sure the programs are running whenever your computer is connected to the Internet. Scan any shared files and downloads with your security software before opening the files. If your security software detects malware, delete it immediately.

ACCESS BY INTERNET SERVICE PROVIDERS

Private information may be accessed and/or disseminated intentionally or accidentally by a subscriber's Internet Service Provider (ISP).

For example, the ISP often downloads graphics and program upgrades to the subscriber's computer, however, a message is usually sent to the subscriber alerting them to the download of such information. Nevertheless, certain ISPs have admitted to inadvertently, and sometimes intentionally, accessing information from the subscriber's computer without their knowledge or consent, purportedly to enhance customer service.

In addition, most ISPs publish online member directories that may contain a subscriber's personal information. Some ISPs sell their member lists to marketing services. However, an ISP will generally remove a subscriber's name and information from their list upon request.

ISP Access to E-mail

Most ISPs offer some mechanism by which a subscriber can send a personal, private message to another, e.g., via e-mail. Viewing or disclosing such messages are generally protected under the Electronic Communications Privacy Act (ECPA), as discussed below. However, there are a number of exceptions to this provision.

For example, the ISP is permitted to view private e-mails if they believe the sender intends to damage the computer system or harm another user. In addition, the ISP is permitted to view and disclose private e-mails if they have the consent from either the sender or recipient of the message. Such consent may have automatically been given in the initial agreement between the subscriber and the ISP.

In addition, certain "enhanced" e-mail messages may contain a graphic called a "web bug," which enables a third party to monitor who is reading the message, confirm when it is read, and record the IP address of the viewer, a multi-digit number that uniquely identifies the viewer's computer. There are software programs available that can detect web bugs.

E-mail is discussed more fully in Chapter 2, "E-mail and Internet Scams," of this Almanac.

Electronic Communications Privacy Act

The Electronic Communications Privacy Act of 1986 (ECPA) [18 U.S.C. § 2510(11)] was enacted by Congress to extend government restrictions on wiretaps from telephone calls to include transmissions of electronic data by computer. Basically, the ECPA protects one's communications from: (1) government surveillance that is conducted without a court order; (2) the unauthorized access by third parties; and (3) access by Internet Service Providers.

Title I protects wire, oral, and electronic communications while in transit. Title II protects communication held in electronic storage, such as messages stored on computers. Title III prohibits the use of trap and trace devices to record dialing, routing, addressing, and signaling information used in the process of transmitting wire or electronic communications without a search warrant.

Selected provisions of the Electronic Communications Privacy Act can be found in Appendix 1, "The Electronic Communications Privacy Act," of this Almanac.

PUBLIC FORUMS

If you participate in a public activity, such as a public forum or newsgroup, the information posted is open to the public. Messages and comments can generally be viewed by anyone with Internet access, and those postings often include the user's screen name, e-mail address and Internet Service Provider.

Further, one may think that, by entering a "chatroom," their online conversation is private. However, any individual in that chat room can copy the content of any other individual's online conversation and disseminate it at will over the Internet. This is so even if entry to the forum or chat room is restricted to members with passwords.

In addition, if a user posts a message in an online newsletter or listserve—an online mailing list that allows individuals or organizations to send e-mail to groups of people at one time—their message will be read by all members of the group. If the user wants to reply privately, they must send the message to that individual's specific e-mail address, and not the address of the newsletter or listserve.

Social networking is discussed more fully in Chapter 6, "Socializing on the Internet," of this Almanac.

THE RISK OF "COOKIES"

Many websites deposit data about a user's visit to the site—e.g., their name, address, and preferences—on the hard drive of the user's computer, so that they can identify the user when he or she returns to visit the site without the user having to reenter the information. The website might also offer products tailored to the user's interests, based on the recorded preferences. The data is stored in the form of small text files known as "cookies."

Although most cookies are used only by the website that placed the data on the user's computer, some cookies—called "third-party" cookies—may transmit the user's data to an advertising clearinghouse which may in turn share that data with other online marketers.

Recording an Internet user's preferences and browsing patterns is a valuable marketing device used by website hosts. They use the information to target potential customers and create "mailing lists." This can result in numerous unsolicited e-mails, generally referred to as "spam."

Internet users who prefer not to have cookies stored on their hard drive can delete the data using their web browser or certain software products designed to detect cookies.

Information on detecting and deleting cookies can be found in Chapter 3, "E-Commerce," of this Almanac.

DOMAIN REGISTRATION SERVICES

Many Internet users obtain their own website name, known as a "domain name." Domain registrations are public information and anyone can look up information about the owner of a domain name online by using certain online services. Currently, the Internet Coalition for Assigned Names and Numbers (ICANN), the agency which coordinates the assignment of Internet domain names, generally requires publication of the mailing address, phone number, and e-mail address of a domain name owner in the "WHOIS" directory.

This policy enables identity thieves, spammers, and other ill-intentioned individuals to obtain the personal information of domain name owners. If possible, you should not provide your personal information when registering a domain name. A number of domain name registrars offer domain privacy as a service to customers. Under this service, when a "WHOIS" search is undertaken to determine the owner of a domain name, the information from a proxy service is provided instead. Nevertheless, the registrar still maintains the personal information of the actual owner, therefore, it is not possible to achieve absolute anonymity.

In addition, owners of certain domains are not permitted to keep their information private. For example, pursuant to the National Telecommunications and Information Administration (NTIA), an agency of the United States Department of Commerce, all owners of ".US" domains must make their information public.

Every country in the world has a two-letter domain allocated to it. The ".US" domain is the official two-letter country code for the USA that, until recently, was a restricted "top level" domain. However, ICANN recently made the ".US" domain available for lower level domain names. Now, any U.S. citizen or resident, as well as any business or organization, including federal, state, and local government with a bona fide presence in the United States can register a ".US" domain name. However, as set forth above, owners of ".US" domain names cannot remain anonymous.

EMPLOYER ACCESS

Employers who operate e-mail systems are allowed to monitor the content of employee e-mails on their system. Therefore, employees have no expectation of privacy in the e-mails they send from an employer-owned e-mail system. This is so even if the e-mail is sent from the employee's home, because a copy is still stored on the employer's main computer server.

Those who use e-mail systems at work are advised to obtain a separate account for their personal e-mail. This would allow the user to check their personal messages without using the workplace e-mail server. Some private accounts can be configured to enable the user to check their personal mail from work without downloading it onto their company's computer.

LAW ENFORCEMENT ACCESS

The Privacy Protection Act of 1980

Congress enacted the Privacy Protection Act of 1980 (PPA) to prohibit the unrestricted search and seizure of materials possessed by publishers. Under the PPA, government officials or employees are prohibited from searching or seizing any work product or documentary materials held by "a person reasonably believed to have a purpose to disseminate to the public a newspaper, book, broadcast, or other similar form of public communication," unless there is probable cause to believe that the person possessing the material has committed or is committing the criminal offense to which the materials relate; or there is reason to believe that the immediate seizure of the material is necessary to prevent the death of, or serious bodily injury to, a human being.

Thus the Act requires law enforcement officials to use subpoenas to obtain evidence from persons engaged in First Amendment activities. Arguably, the PPA extends protection to online activities, such as e-mail, bulletin boards, chat rooms, etc., pursuant to the "other form of public communication" clause of the Act.

The Privacy Protection Act of 1980 can be found in Appendix 2, "The Privacy Protection Act of 1980," of this Almanac.

The U.S. Patriot Act Reauthorized

Internet Service Providers must honor court orders or subpoenas that request disclosure of the private information of their subscribers. However, since the terrorist attacks of September 11th, law enforcement access to online activities has been greatly expanded pursuant to the U.S. Patriot Act, which was passed by Congress in November 2001, and reauthorized in February 2006.

For example, various provisions under Title II of the Act allow for the disclosure of electronic communications to law enforcement agencies that would have previously required a court order. In addition, those who operate or own a "protected computer" can give permission for authorities to intercept communications carried out on the machine, thus bypassing the more stringent requirements of the Wiretap laws.

Selected provisions of the U.S. Patriot Act can be found in Appendix 3, "U.S.A. Patriot Act— Selected Provisions," of this Almanac.

PRIVACY LEGISLATION AND ADVOCACY

Numerous privacy laws have been enacted by federal and state governments, in large part due to computer technology and the changes in information gathering that have occurred over the past twenty years. The laws vary, but their common goal is to protect individuals from the unauthorized use of the collected information and government access to private records.

A summary of federal privacy laws can be found in Appendix 4, "Summary of Federal Privacy Laws," and a summary of state privacy laws can be found in Appendix 5.

In addition, there are many organizations dedicated to assisting the Internet user in maintaining the privacy of their personal information. These organizations offer advice and guidance on Internet usage and privacy issues, and many are advocates who lobby the government for more stringent privacy legislation. Their websites provide a host of information on the practical and legal issues concerning privacy on the Internet.

An Internet privacy resource directory can be found in Appendix 6, "Internet Privacy Resource Directory," of this Almanac.

PRIVACY POLICIES

Companies operating online often ask their customers personal information so that they can gather marketing information concerning the people who visit their website. The information gathered may also be shared with others for marketing and other purposes. Privacy policies vary among websites, therefore, the consumer is advised to read them carefully.

It is important to determine whether the website you visit has a privacy policy. If so, the privacy policy should detail the following:

1. the type of information collected;

2. how the information is used;

3. whether the information is shared with third parties; and

4. what control the consumer has over their personal information.

Privacy policies also should tell the consumer how they can find out what information has been collected by the website so that erroneous information can be corrected or deleted. The privacy policy should also explain how the company restricts their employees' access to the consumer's personal information.

Consumers may also have the choice to "opt out" of having their information used in various ways. If there is such an "opt out" policy, the consumer must generally affirmatively state that they do not want their information used. Otherwise, the information will be disseminated, meaning that it will be used unless you say "no." If there is an "opt in" policy, this means that the consumer's personal information cannot be used unless they affirmatively state that they want their information used.

Many websites also ask the consumer's permission to contact them in the future by e-mail with notices, updates, offers and other information. The consumer should have the option of declining permission for future contact.

Privacy policies are discussed more fully in Chapter 3, "E-Commerce," of this Almanac.

THE ROLE OF THE FEDERAL TRADE COMMISSION

The Federal Trade Commission (FTC) Bureau of Consumer Protection is the nation's primary consumer protection organization. The Division of Privacy and Identity Protection is the newest of the Bureau's divisions.

Enforcement of Privacy Rights

The Division oversees issues related to consumer privacy, credit reporting, identity theft, and information security. It also enforces the laws within its jurisdiction. One such law that relates to consumer privacy and information security is the Gramm-Leach-Bliley Act (the "Safeguards Rule"), which was enacted in 1999.

The Act requires financial institutions to ensure the security and confidentiality of customer information, provide notice to consumers about their information practices, and give consumers an opportunity to direct that their personal information not be shared with certain non-affiliated third parties.

The Division has undertaken enforcement efforts to ensure that financial institutions comply with the law and has implemented an outreach program to increase consumer awareness of the notices.

The Gramm-Leach-Bliley Act is discussed further in Chapter 4, "Online Financial Services," of this Almanac.

Privacy Initiatives

Since the expansion of the Internet, the need to educate consumers and businesses about the importance of personal information privacy, including the security of personal information, has become an utmost priority for the Division. The Division actively investigates privacy violations and aggressively enforces the nation's privacy laws. The Division has also developed a number of privacy initiatives, as discussed below.

Anti-Spam Enforcement Initiative

As further discussed in this Almanac, junk e-mail, known as spam, presents serious safety concerns for consumers as well as a tremendous burden on the Internet. Spam e-mail often contains deceptive and fraudulent schemes, such as chain letters, pyramid schemes and other types of scams intended to victimize unsophisticated Internet users. The FTC is increasing its enforcement activities against these illegal activities.

Identity Theft Prevention Initiative

Identity theft is a swiftly growing national problem due, in large part, to the ability of identity thieves to access an individual's personal identifying information through the Internet. As further discussed in this Almanac, identity theft can ruin a consumer's credit and make it difficult, if not impossible, for the victim to get a loan, rent an apartment or even get a job.

The Division oversees the Identity Theft Data Clearinghouse, which administers the federal government's centralized database for consumer identity theft complaints. The Division analyzes identity theft trends and promotes the development of identity fraud prevention strategies in the financial services industry. The Division also operates a call center for ID theft victims where counselors tell consumers how to protect themselves from identity theft and what to do if their identity has been stolen.

Identity theft prevention is discussed more fully in Chapter 7, "Internet Identity Theft," of this Almanac.

Anti-Pretexting Initiative

"Pretexting" is the practice of fraudulently obtaining an individual's personal financial information, such as account numbers and balances, by contacting financial institutions under the pretext of being a customer. Pretexting is prohibited by the Gramm-Leach-Bliley Act. The Division actively investigates this practice, seeks injunctions against offenders, and aggressively enforces the law.

The Division works to make sure that all participants in the credit reporting system meet their obligations regarding the accuracy of a consumer's credit information. The Division also requires that consumers be notified when information in a credit report is the reason for a denial of credit, insurance or employment.

Privacy Promises Enforcement Initiative

Companies with whom consumers do business make privacy promises to their customers. The Division has encouraged websites to post privacy notices and honor the promises made and, as a result, many websites now post their privacy policies online. The Division also brings enforcement actions against companies that fail to honor the promises found in their privacy statements.

Children's Online Privacy Initiative

As further discussed in this Almanac, The Children's Online Privacy Protection Act of 1998 (COPPA) prevents the collection of personally identifiable information from children without their parent's consent. The FTC enforces the provisions of COPPA, and provides educational materials to parents concerning their children's online activities.

COPPA is discussed more fully in Chapter 5, "Protecting Children's Privacy Online," of this Almanac.

Privacy Complaints Hotline

The Division operates a toll-free hotline number (1-877-FTC-HELP) as well as a complaint form on its website (www.ftc.gov) for consumers to report privacy-related complaints, as well as fraudulent and deceptive business practices. The FTC enters Internet, telemarketing, identity theft, and other fraud-related complaints into Consumer Sentinel, a secure, online database available to hundreds of civil and criminal law enforcement agencies in the U.S. and overseas.

CHAPTER 2:
E-MAIL AND INTERNET SCAMS

IN GENERAL

Internet users communicate with each other online using e-mail and instant messaging. It is an immediate way of transmitting information to others, and has become very popular as a means of communication in both personal and business affairs. Unfortunately, as set forth below, communicating online does not afford the same level of privacy that written correspondence offers.

SECURING E-MAIL

E-mail is a way of communicating electronically from one computer to another computer. All kinds of information can be sent via e-mail, including text messages, letters, documents, music, pictures, etc.

Encryption

E-mail is generally not secure and can be intercepted and read by others. Therefore, it would be unwise to transmit any personal identifying or financial information in an e-mail unless you use e-mail cryptography software to scramble your messages in code. Encryption is a method of scrambling an e-mail message or file so that it is gibberish to anyone who does not know how to unscramble it.

The privacy advantage of encryption is that anything encrypted is virtually inaccessible to anyone other than the designated recipient. Thus private information may be encrypted and then transmitted, stored, or distributed without fear that it will be read by others.

Anonymous Remailers

Anonymous remailers were created to address privacy risks and concerns by allowing the user to send anonymous e-mail messages. An anonymous remailer is a special e-mail server that acts as a middleman and strips outgoing e-mail of all personally identifying information, then forwards it to its destination, usually with the IP address of the remailer attached.

Deleting Stored E-mail

Every time an e-mail message is sent, a number of copies of that e-mail message are created. One copy is stored locally on the sender's computer, another on the sender's ISP's system, another on the recipient's computer, and one copy is stored on the recipient's ISP's system. You can delete the stored copy of your e-mail by opening the "sent mail" folder in the e-mail program and delete the e-mail by removing it to the trash folder, and then emptying the trash folder.

Web-Based E-mail Service

Another way of keeping e-mail private when you share a computer is to use a web-based e-mail service. Web-based e-mail services store the user's e-mail on a computer server, such as a web page, instead of the user's computer. Again, make sure you keep your password private.

Employer Access

As explained in Chapter 1, "Securing Your Computer," employers are legally allowed to view and monitor any e-mails on the employer's e-mail system, even if the e-mail is sent from the employee's home. Therefore, employees who use the employer's e-mail system are advised to obtain a separate account for their personal e-mail, which would allow the employee to check their personal messages without using the workplace e-mail server.

E-mail Forwarding

Recipients of an e-mail can forward that e-mail to an unlimited number of additional recipients with the simple click of the mouse. The sender has no control over how many people ultimately view the e-mail he or she sends. If you don't want the e-mail you send to be viewed by an unlimited number of people, you must send it to someone who you can trust will not forward it without your consent.

Identity Verification

The nature of e-mail makes it difficult to verify that the person who signs the e-mail is the actual person who is sending the e-mail. With regular mail, you can generally identify the sender by their handwriting, the signature, or the letterhead on which the correspondence is sent. However, you cannot identify an individual from the font type they use to create the e-mail.

Thus it is possible to unwittingly correspond with a complete stranger who is pretending to be someone known to you. Nevertheless, there is software available on the market that can assist senders and recipients of e-mails with the identification process, such as the digital signature.

E-MAIL VIRUSES

From time to time, the media reports on "viruses" that are circulating in cyberspace, such as the infamous "Melissa" virus. A virus can do considerable damage to computer programs and files and can also reveal personal information stored on the computer.

To protect yourself from accidentally downloading a virus to your computer, do not open any e-mail attachments from unknown senders. Even if you are familiar with the sender, if the subject matter appears suspicious, do not open it. Those who circulate these viruses are able to access a computer user's address book and e-mail the virus so that it appears to be coming from a known sender.

Also be aware that certain programs available for download on the Internet may contain viruses. Check out the particular download carefully before opening it. As explained in Chapter 1, "Securing Your Computer," it is advisable to install and regularly update anti-virus software on your computer that will search for viruses and alert you to their presence so that they can be immediately deleted.

SPAM E-MAIL

Most Internet users are bombarded with numerous unsolicited junk e-mail messages from businesses and individuals seeking to market their products, services and scams over the Internet. These e-mails are known as "spam."

A business or individual will generally buy a list of e-mail addresses from a third party, and then use software that allows them to send messages to everyone on the list within seconds. The harvesting of e-mail addresses is generally automated. Spam e-mail finds its way to new e-mail addresses soon after they are used publicly for the first time.

Spam Reduction Tactics

As set forth below, there are a number of methods designed to reduce the amount of unsolicited e-mail messages.

Do Not Publicize Your E-mail Address

Since the individuals who compile the lists of e-mail addresses harvest those addresses from the Internet, you should try not to display their e-mail address publicly over the Internet. You should also request that your Internet service provider remove your name from membership directories that are posted on the Internet. In addition, you should try not to publish your e-mail address in chat rooms and on websites.

Mask Your E-mail Address

Masking involves putting a word or phrase in your e-mail address so that it will generally trick a harvesting computer program, but not a person. For example, if your e-mail address is "johndoe@myisp.com," you could mask it as "johndoe@spamaway.myisp.com."

However, some newsgroup services or message boards won't allow you to mask your e-mail address and some harvesting programs may be able to pick out common masks.

Use Two E-mail Addresses

Many websites require the user to provide their e-mail address before they can sign up for online services or purchase products online. In that case, it might be prudent to use two e-mail addresses and designate one for personal use and one for public use on the Internet. If you use chat rooms, use a screen name that's not associated with your e-mail address. Consider using the screen name only for online chat.

Use a Disposable E-mail Address

There are services that provide Internet users with "disposable" e-mail addresses that forward e-mail to the permanent e-mail account. Then, if one of the disposable addresses begins to receive spam e-mail, the user can turn it off without affecting their permanent address.

Create a Unique E-mail Address

Another method of trying to avoid being spammed is to create a unique e-mail address. Your choice of e-mail address may affect the amount of spam you receive. Some spammers use "dictionary attacks" to e-mail many possible name combinations at large ISPs or e-mail services, trying to come up with common names and variations to locate valid e-mail addresses in order to compile a list.

For example, marysmith@aol.com and variations of this e-mail address are very easy for a spammer to validate. It is much more difficult to try and decode an e-mail address that is randomly made up of numbers and letters.

Filter Junk E-mail

Many e-mail systems have screening capabilities that allow the user to limit the amount of unsolicited commercial e-mail that ends up in the user's inbox. Junk mail filters use certain criteria to filter out junk mail. For example, junk mail filters identify items such as font style, symbols, and phrasing to classify messages as junk mail.

The junk mail is then diverted to another folder, according to the user's preferences. Junk mail may be sent directly to the trash, or to a bulk e-mail folder, where it generally remains for a certain amount of time before being automatically deleted. The user can view the contents of the folder at any time to make sure the junk mail filter is not eliminating e-mails that the user may want to receive.

Check Out Website Privacy Policies

In addition, it is important to check the privacy policy for any website you visit and find out whether the company sells or shares its visitors' identifying information before submitting your personal information. If the privacy policy indicates that the company does compile such information, it is best not to visit that website or you risk opening yourself up to more unsolicited commercial e-mail. Some websites allow the user to "opt out" of receiving e-mail from third parties if the user so chooses.

Register for an E-mail Preference Service

Another way of reducing the amount of unsolicited commercial e-mail is to register for the e-Mail Preference Service (e-MPS) offered by the Direct Marketing Association (www.e-mps.org). All DMA members who wish to send unsolicited commercial e-mail must delete from their e-mail prospecting lists the names of any individuals who have registered their e-mail address with e-MPS. The service is also available to non-DMA members.

The CAN-SPAM Act of 2003 (Pub. L. No. 108-187)

In 2003, Congress enacted the Controlling the Assault of Non-Solicited Pornography and Marketing Act of 2003, commonly referred to as the CAN-SPAM Act of 2003.

The CAN-SPAM Act contains a number of important provisions that are designed to deter and punish those who seek to send spam. The Act amends the federal criminal code to impose a fine, imprisonment, or both, on any person who:

1. accesses a protected computer without authorization and intentionally initiates the transmission of multiple commercial electronic mail messages from or through such computer;

2. uses a protected computer to relay or retransmit multiple messages, with the intent to deceive or mislead recipients or any Internet access service as to the origin of such messages;

3. materially falsifies header information in multiple messages and intentionally initiates the transmission thereof;

4. registers, with materially false identifying information, for five or more electronic mail accounts or online user accounts or two or more domain names, and intentionally initiates the transmission of multiple messages from such accounts or domain names; or

5. falsely represents oneself to be the registrant or legitimate successor in interest to the registrant of five or more Internet protocol addresses and intentionally initiates the transmission of multiple messages from such addresses.

The Act also provides for higher penalties in the case of offenses committed in furtherance of any felony, or if the defendant has previously been convicted for conduct involving the transmission of multiple messages or unauthorized access to a computer system. The violator may also be required to forfeit any property obtained from such an offense, and the equipment, software, or other technology used to commit the offense.

The Act sets forth protections against spam that include the following:

1. a prohibition against false or misleading transmission information;

2. a prohibition against deceptive subject headings;

3. mandatory inclusion of a return address or a comparable mechanism in commercial electronic mail;

4. a prohibition against transmission of spam after objection, including a prohibition against transferring or releasing an e-mail address after an objection;

5. mandatory inclusion in spam of information identifying the message as an advertisement or solicitation, notice of the opportunity to decline to receive further unsolicited messages from the sender, and the sender's physical address;

6. a prohibition against initiating transmission of spam to a protected computer, or assisting in the origination of such message through the provision of addresses, if the person had actual knowledge, or knowledge fairly implied on the basis of objective circumstances, that the recipient's address was obtained from an Internet website or proprietary online service that included a notice that the operator will not provide addresses for initiating unsolicited messages;

7. a prohibition against using automated means to register for multiple e-mail accounts for the transmission of spam; and

8. a prohibition against relaying or retransmitting an unsolicited message that is unlawful under this section.

Selected provisions of the CAN-SPAM Act can be found in Appendix 7, "The CAN-SPAM Act of 2003—Selected Provision," of this Almanac.

COMMON E-MAIL SCAMS

Many consumers have lost thousands of dollars in deceptive e-mail scams. According to the FTC, many unsolicited e-mail messages contain false information about the sender and/or misleading subject lines, and extravagant earnings or performance claims about goods and services. This widespread ability to disseminate false and misleading claims is the FTC's main concern with spam e-mail.

As discussed below, common deceptive spam e-mail scams that you may encounter include "phishing" e-mails; illegal chain letters; work-at-home schemes; credit repair offers; advance-fee loan offers; fraudulent ISP messages; and fraudulent adult entertainment invitations.

Phishing E-mails

The term "phishing" refers to a type of deception designed to steal a computer user's valuable personal data, such as credit card numbers, passwords, account data, social security number, financial records, or other information. Phishing is typically carried out using e-mail. The e-mail appears to be coming from a trusted website.

Chain E-mails

Chain letters used to be sent by regular mail, however, since the inception of the Internet, they are now being circulated via "chain e-mails." Chain e-mails generally include a list of names and addresses with instructions to send money to one or more names on a list. The recipient is then instructed to remove one or more names from the list, add their name to the bottom of the list, and e-mail the letter to a certain number of other people with directions on how to "continue the chain" in order for the recipient to receive his or her share of the money. The sender may also state that the chain e-mails are legal.

According to the FTC, chain e-mails are not legal and those who start, send or forward chain e-mail messages are breaking the law and can be prosecuted for mail fraud. Recipients of chain e-mails are advised to file a complaint with their Internet Service Provider and report the offer to the FTC, or to their State Consumer Protection Office.

A directory of State Consumer Protection Agencies can be found in Appendix 8, "Directory of State Consumer Protection Agenices," of this Almanac.

Work-at-Home Scam

There are many work-at-home scams circulating on the Internet. These "opportunities" usually require the "employee" to pay certain costs to get the home business up and running, such as tutorial software and manuals. In some cases, the individual works many hours without pay, or spends their own money on postage, envelopes, photocopies, etc., and never get paid for their out-of-pocket expenses or their efforts. Many individuals who have responded to these scams have ended up losing thousands of dollars in addition to wasting valuable time and energy on a fruitless venture.

Credit Repair Offers

Another e-mail scam involves an offer to repair your credit and rid your credit report of negative information. Be aware that there is no legal way to delete accurate negative information from your credit report. Do not respond to these e-mails.

Advance Fee Loan Scam

If you receive an e-mail promising to give you a loan for a fee, regardless of your credit history, ignore it. Legitimate lenders do not issue credit cards or provide loans without first making sure you are qualified and have a decent credit rating.

Nigerian Advance-Fee Scam

According to the FTC, the Nigerian advance-fee fraud scheme has reached epidemic proportions, with some Internet users reportedly receiving dozens of these fraudulent offers each day. The e-mails are purportedly sent from Nigerians officials or businessmen who promise financial rewards for assistance in moving large sums of money out of their country. Those who respond to the offer may receive documents that appear official and are asked to provide bank account numbers and a fee to cover costs. After getting as much money out of the victim as possible, the con artists disappear.

Internet Service Provider Scam

A common scam designed to obtain personal financial information from the consumer involves e-mail requests purportedly sent from the consumer's Internet service provider (ISP). The e-mail request generally advises the consumer that "your account information needs to be updated" or that "the credit card you signed up with is invalid or expired and the information needs to be reentered to keep your account active." Consumers are advised not to respond to any such e-mail request without first checking with their ISP.

Adult Entertainment Invitation Scam

An e-mail from an adult entertainment website may invite you to download a program that permits you to view the content of the website for free without providing a credit card. Be suspicious of any such "free" offer. It has been reported that once the program is downloaded onto the computer, the program disconnects the Internet connection and reconnects to an international long distance phone number, charging rates between $2 and $7 per minute.

Government Rebate Check Scam

Scam artists are always looking for new schemes to make money. According to the FTC, they follow the headlines in order to find ways to exploit innocent citizens. The latest ploy reported involved the government's plan to send stimulus payments to consumers.

Scammers claiming to be from the Internal Revenue Service or the Social Security Administration call or send an e-mail asking for information to be able to deposit your rebate check directly into your bank account. They may ask for a checking account number, social security number, or other type of personal information, which can be used to commit identity theft. The FTC advises consumers not to give out personal or financial information in response to an unsolicited call or e-mail.

The IRS does not send unsolicited e-mails to taxpayers about tax account matters. If you receive an e-mail from someone claiming to be from the IRS that asks you to e-mail them with your personal information, don't click on any links. Clicking on a link in an unsolicited e-mail carries risks of malware and phishing—threats that can lead to the theft of your identity, as discussed above. Simply forward the e-mail to the IRS website set up for this purpose (phishing@irs.gov/). After you have forwarded the e-mail, delete it.

Similarly, the SSA does not send unsolicited e-mails. Again, if you receive an e-mail from someone claiming to be from the SSA and it asks for your personal information, do not respond or click any links in the e-mail. Delete the e-mail and report the scam to the SSA.

FILING A COMPLAINT

The Federal Trade Commission (FTC)

The Federal Trade Commission (FTC) advises Internet users to forward unsolicited or deceptive e-mail messages to their e-mail address designated for this purpose (spam@uce.gov). The FTC uses the unsolicited e-mails stored in this database to pursue law enforcement actions against those who send deceptive spam e-mail.

In addition, you should also notify the FTC if your request to remove your address from a mailing list is not honored. The FTC has an online complaint form for this purpose on its website (www.ftc.gov). Each complaint is added to the FTC's Consumer Sentinel database and made available to hundreds of law enforcement and consumer protection agencies.

When making a complaint, it is important to include the full e-mail header of the spam e-mail. The information in the header makes it possible for the FTC to follow up on the complaint.

Your Internet Service Provider

You should also send a copy of the unsolicited e-mail to the abuse desk of your Internet Service Provider (ISP). Often the e-mail address is abuse@yourispname.com or postmaster@yourispname.com. Include a copy of the spam, along with the full e-mail header, and at the top of the message, state that you're complaining about being spammed. Forwarding your spam to your ISP lets them know about the spam problem on their system and helps them to stop it.

The Sender's Internet Service Provider

A complaint should also be made with the abuse desk of the sender's ISP. Most ISPs want to stop spammers who abuse their system. Include a copy of the message and the full e-mail header information, and state that you're complaining about spam.

INSTANT MESSAGING

Instant messaging is the ability to communicate with another on the Internet in a chat-like mode. Generally, the user sets up their instant messaging network so that they are notified when an individual on their list is online. They can then send an instant message to that person, who can respond immediately on screen. It is much like talking on the telephone, except the parties type their messages back and forth.

As a privacy feature, most instant message programs allow users to be invisible to all other users except those selected to appear on their instant messaging list.

CHAPTER 3:
E-COMMERCE

IN GENERAL

Consumers are increasingly using the Internet to shop, bank and invest online. The Internet has brought the international marketplace into American homes. There are online stores offering unique products from all over the world. However, this increase in online shopping underscores the need for security and privacy of online transactions. In fact, privacy and security are the two most important reasons some consumers are reluctant to shop online.

To minimize your risks, you must ensure that the company with whom you plan to do business is legitimate. The following precautions should be taken in order to avoid online fraud and the interception of personal information:

1. Patronize websites of reputable, familiar companies, such as companies who also operate retail stores or mail order catalogues.

2. Patronize companies that display a privacy seal on their website, and read the website's privacy statement to determine their privacy practices.

3. Make sure the company has a physical address and a telephone number so that they can be contacted off-line. A company that lists a post office box instead of a physical address, or one that discloses no contact information, may be a fly-by-night operation set up for illegal purposes.

4. Check with the state Attorney General's Office to see whether there are any adverse reports about the particular company.

5. Give out only the amount of information that is necessary for you to complete the online transaction.

6. When dealing with an unfamiliar company, start out by purchasing a small, inexpensive item to determine how the company handles the order.

7. Use a unique password when registering on a site, randomly combining letters and numbers, and never disclose the password to anyone.

8. Do not send private information by e-mail.

9. Check to make sure you are actually on the official website of the company you want to patronize. Criminals have been known to create websites with names similar to legitimate businesses in order to intercept personal information. One way of checking the legitimacy of a website is to visit http://www.whois.net, a service which sets forth the identity of the registrant of the URL, and the physical address of the company.

10. Often companies hold contests in order to collect names and contact information for future marketing. When deciding whether to enter a contest, consider whether you want the company operating the contest to have access to your personal information.

11. Opt-out of third party information sharing by requesting that a company remove your name from any lists of information that may be shared with third parties.

SECURING ONLINE PAYMENTS

Method of Payment

Credit and Debit Cards

Most online shoppers use credit cards to pay for their online purchases. However, debit cards are increasing in use. Your debit card may be an automated teller machine (ATM) card that can be used for retail purchases. To complete a debit card transaction, you may have to use a personal identification number (PIN), some form of a signature or other identification, or a combination of these identifiers. Some cards have both credit and debit features: you select the payment option at the point-of-sale.

It is important to note that, although a debit card may look like a credit card, the money for debit purchases is transferred almost immediately from your bank account to the merchant's account. In addition, your liability limits for a lost or stolen debit card and unauthorized use are different from your liability if your credit card is lost, stolen, or used without your authorization.

E-Money

In order to make purchasing easier, some merchants accept "electronic money" or "e-money." An example of "e-money" is a "stored-value" card that lets you transfer cash value to the card. Some stored-value cards contain computer chips that make them "smart" cards. Smart cards may act like a credit card as well as a debit card, and may also contain stored value.

E-Wallets

Some merchants allow value to be transmitted through computers, commonly referred to as "e-wallets." You can use an "e-wallet" to make a "micropayment"—i.e., a very small online or offline payment for things like a magazine or fast food.

When you buy something using your e-wallet, the balance on your online account decreases by that amount. "E-wallets" may work by using some form of stored value or by automatically accessing an account you've set up through a computer system connected to your credit or debit card account.

Review the Website Security System

In order to make sure that your payments are securely processed, and your credit card information is not exposed to potential identity thieves, you should review the company's payment security policies before purchasing the merchandise you order. Before giving out credit card information, it is important to verify the website's online security or encryption capabilities.

To determine the type of security system a website uses, you should read the website's privacy statement, as discussed below. Many websites use Secure Sockets Layer (SSL) technology to encrypt the credit card information that the consumer sends over the Internet. One way of determining whether or not a website is using such technology is to watch the address bar on the screen. At the point where the consumer enters their personal information, such as a credit card number, the prefix on the address should change from "http" to "shttp" or "https."

A different security technology, which works on different principles, is Secure Electronic Transaction (SET) technology, which was developed by MasterCard and Visa. SET assures secure credit and charge card payment using highly encrypted communication between card issuers, merchants, and card members. SET also provides an enhanced level of security, confidentiality, and transaction integrity. Both SSL and SET technology are designed to make the connection secure.

You can also determine whether a website uses security software if the browser displays the icon of a locked padlock at the bottom of the screen or if there is an icon of an unbroken key at the bottom of the screen; or if there is an icon of a lock on the status bar.

Secure Your Personal Information

Although it may be impossible to protect yourself completely from fraud and deception in both online and off-line purchases, there are some steps you can take to make it less likely your personal information will be intercepted, as further discussed below.

Use a Secure Browser

A browser is special software that allows the consumer to navigate through the Internet and view various websites. Most computers come with some type of browser installed, e.g., Internet Explorer and Netscape Navigator. Some browsers are available for downloading on the Internet at no cost. Browsers transmit a consumer's personal information to website operators, including but not limited to the consumer's Internet Service Provider, and websites the consumer has visited.

When providing personal identifying or financial information online, you must use a secure browser. A secure browser refers to software that encrypts or scrambles the purchase information sent over the Internet. You should be sure that the browser you use has the latest encryption capabilities available and should comply with industry security standards.

If the company website states that your personal identifying or financial information does not need to be encrypted, you should not patronize the website. When submitting your purchase information, look for the "lock" icon on the browser's status bar, and the phrase "https" in the URL address for a website, to be sure your information is secure during transmission.

Empty the Cache

The "cache" is an area on the computer's hard drive where copies of the websites you visit are stored so that the browser can access them locally instead of going to the website. This helps to make browsing faster and easier. However, storing your browsing record can jeopardize your privacy, particularly if you share the computer with others, or use a public computer, e.g., in a library or Internet cafe.

To minimize security risks, you should delete this information. The browsing record can be deleted by following your browser's instructions for "emptying the cache," and then closing the browser.

Cookies

"Cookies" are bits of electronic information in the form of small text files that identify the computer used by a specific customer to a particular website. Cookies are placed on a computer's hard drive when you visit various websites. Cookies are used by the website to tailor information to a particular customer, such as marketing information, preferences, etc. This data may include your name, address, preferences, and browsing patterns.

Cookies inform the website operator when you have visited the website, and can be used to track your online activity, and enable the website operator to create a profile for you without your knowledge. If you obtained a username and password to access the website, cookies remembers that information so that you can easily access the website again without having to enter your password each time you visit the site. When you revisit the same website, the cookie file is opened and the stored information is accessed.

Third Party Cookies

Although most cookies are used only by the website that placed the data on your computer, some cookies—called third-party cookies—are maintained by websites other than the one you visited. Third-party cookies may transmit your personal information and online activity to an advertising clearinghouse that may in turn share that data with other online marketers. This can lead to many unsolicited commercial e-mails being sent to you.

Detecting Cookies and Setting Preferences

The presence of cookies on your hard drive can be detected using special software or particular browser settings. You can search the hard drive for a file with the word "cookie" in it—e.g., cookie.txt—to view the cookies that have been stored on your computer.

If you prefer not to allow a website to place cookies on your computer's hard drive, you can change your preferences setting concerning the manner in which cookies are stored. For example, you can choose to limit third-party cookies, or you can completely disable the ability for cookies to be placed on your hard drive.

Newer browsers allow the consumer to recognize websites that send cookies in advance. The consumer can then reject the cookies before they are placed on the computer's hard drive rather than having to delete them afterwards.

Anonymous Remailers

Consumers who are reluctant to provide any personal information online may use a program that masks their identity, such as an "anonymous remailer," by enabling the consumer to make their online transactions through third parties.

PRIVACY STATEMENTS

In General

When you place an order for merchandise over the Internet, the company will require certain personal information in order to process your order, such as your name, address, e-mail address, telephone number, etc. You should review the company's privacy statement, which should be clearly stated on their website. In fact, it is advisable to read the privacy statements of all the websites with which you do business, including the privacy statement of your own Internet Service Provider.

Some company's privacy statements are easier to find than others. The link to a company's privacy statement may be located at the bottom of the website home page; on the order form; or in the "About Us" or "FAQs" section of a website. If you're not comfortable with the information contained in the policy statement, consider doing business elsewhere. In any event, you should not patronize a business that does not have a privacy statement posted on their website.

The company's privacy statement should describe the way in which the website collects, shares and protects your personal information, and how the information will be used. A privacy statement is a legally binding document which the website owner must abide by or face legal action.

Some businesses use the information collected to provide you with notice of future sales and promotions. However, other businesses sell or share your personal information to other businesses. You should be given the opportunity to "opt out"—i.e., to prohibit the company from sharing your information with others without your knowledge or consent.

Elements of a Privacy Statement

A website's privacy statement should be easily accessible and understandable. Some websites post a simplified version of their privacy policy that is easy for consumers to read, and provide links to additional information, which may contain more complicated legal or technical information.

A well-drafted privacy policy should provide the consumer with the following information:

1. the information that is being collected;

2. whether the information is personally identifiable;

3. the reasons the website collects the information;

4. the appropriateness of the data collection as it relates to the particular activity or transaction;

5. the manner in which the data is collected;

6. whether the consumer has a choice regarding the type and quantity of personal information that the site collects;

7. whether the website uses cookies;

8. whether the website maintains web logs;

9. how the personal information collected is used by the website;

10. whether personal information is ever used for a secondary purpose—i.e., a purpose other than that for which the consumer has provided the information;

11. if personal information is used for a secondary purpose, the consumer should be so informed;

12. whether the visitor has consented to secondary use of personal information;

13. whether the visitor has the option to prohibit secondary use of personal information;

14. whether the website offers different kinds of service depending on consumer privacy preferences, e.g., does the website disadvantage consumers who exercise data collection choices;

15. whether the consumer can access the information collected;

16. whether the consumer can correct inaccurate data that has been collected;

17. the length of time personal information is stored;

18. the website's complaint procedures;

19. contact information, such as an e-mail address or phone number, so the consumer can contact the company if they have any questions about online security or their privacy policy statement;

20. the laws governing data collection; and

21. whether the website collecting the information is regulated by the Privacy Act or any other privacy law.

Companies should develop privacy statements for their websites that incorporate the elements discussed above.

A sample Internet Privacy Statement Outline can be found in Appendix 9, "Sample Internet Privacy Statement Outline," of this Almanac.

The privacy statement issued by the American Express Company is an example of a well-drafted privacy statement and can be found in Appendix 10, "The American Express Internet Privacy Statement," of this Almanac.

THIRD PARTY AUTHENTICATION SERVICES

In General

Third party authentication services issue "seals" that are displayed on a company's website to demonstrate that the business has complied with certain business practices relating to, among other things, security, and privacy.

These third party seals lend credibility to a company and give certain assurances to customers, depending on the type of seal issued. The most well-known seal programs are operated by TRUSTe and BBBOnline, as further discussed below.

Types of Seals

There are five main categories of seals: (1) reliability seals; (2) security seals; (3) vulnerability seals; (4) privacy seals; and (5) consumer ratings seals.

Reliability Seals

Reliability seals simply vouch for the identity of the company, including their mailing address, telephone number, and e-mail address. These seals do not, however, guarantee the level of service provided by the company nor the manner in which a customer's personal information may be collected or used.

Security Seals

Security seals verify that a company has Secure Socket Layer (SSL) protection for the transmission of sensitive data, as discussed above. However, security seals do not account for the handling of your personal information once the data has been transmitted via SSL technology and has entered the recipient's database.

Vulnerability Seals

Vulnerability seals certify that a third party service monitors the website at various intervals—e.g., daily, weekly, or monthly—searching for any vulnerable areas that may be exploited by hackers into the system.

Privacy Seals

Privacy seals are branded symbols of trust on the Internet similar to the Good Housekeeping "seal of approval." They give added assurance that a website is abiding by its posted privacy statement. Privacy seals demonstrate that a company respectfully uses the personal information you provide.

Privacy seals are the most difficult to obtain, as they require the company to undergo an extensive certification process that exposes internal data collection and usage processes. A privacy seal is the only type of seal that investigates internal and external privacy threats.

Privacy seal programs offer third-party verification and monitoring of the information practices of websites. These programs also operate procedures whereby a customer who believes his or her privacy has been violated by a program participant can file a complaint with the authority that issued the seal, which will work to resolve the problem.

Consumer Ratings Seals

Consumer ratings seals simply provide potential customers with reviews from other customers. While this may be helpful in terms of providing you with an expectation as to the quality of the shopping experience, these seals do not guarantee any degree of security or privacy, as do the foregoing seals.

The TRUSTe Seal Program

TRUSTe is an independent, non-profit initiative to build consumer trust and confidence on the Internet. TRUSTe is responsible for developing the first online privacy seal program. The TRUSTe privacy seal program assures consumers that the websites they visit are compliant with fair information practices approved by the U.S. Department of Commerce, the Federal Trade Commission, and prominent industry-represented organizations and associations.

A website that is a member of the TRUSTe seal program will display a TRUSTe privacy seal on the website's privacy statement. When the consumer clicks on the privacy seal, he or she will be directed to a validation page on the TRUSTe website. If the consumer is not directed to the validation page, the consumer should be aware that the website may be displaying a fraudulent TRUSTe seal.

To verify that a website is a member of the TRUSTe seal program, a consumer can view a list of participants on the TRUSTe website (http://www.truste.org/).

If a consumer believes that a TRUSTe participant has committed a privacy violation, an online complaint—referred to as a "watchdog"—should be filed on the TRUSTe website. TRUSTe will review the complaint and confirm that the website is a TRUSTe participant. TRUSTe can only act on privacy violation complaints, and can only accept complaints about a company that is a participant in the program.

TRUSTe will contact the website and make inquiries about the complaint. TRUSTe may also contact the consumer to get more information about their complaint. TRUSTe will contact the participating company and respond to the consumer within 10 business days. The participating company has 5 days after that to respond to TRUSTe and the consumer.

Depending on the nature of the complaint, TRUSTe may require the participating company to change its privacy statement or privacy practices. TRUSTe will also have the consumer's information corrected, modified, or deleted, as appropriate. A company that refuses to comply with a TRUSTe decision may be referred to the appropriate government agency, removed from the TRUSTe program, and be subject to legal action with TRUSTe. Either party to the complaint may file an appeal of a TRUSTe decision within 10 days of receipt of the decision.

As further discussed in Chapter 5, "Protecting Children's Privacy Online," of this Almanac, TRUSTe also sponsors a Children's Privacy Seal for websites that are directed at children under 13.

BBBOnline Seal Program

BBBOnline is a wholly owned subsidiary of the Council of Better Business Bureaus. Their mission is to promote trust and confidence on the Internet through the BBBOnLine trustmark. BBBOnLine allows companies with websites to display the mark once they have been evaluated and confirmed to meet the program standards for good business practices online.

The BBBOnLine trustmark confirms that a business has been accredited by the BBB where it is based, has been reviewed to meet BBB's truth in advertising guidelines, discloses information about the business and its policies, follows basic privacy and security practices, and responds appropriately to any problems that arise. The BBBOnLine trustmark links to a BBB report on the business, allowing online shoppers to instantly verify a business's trustworthiness.

A website that is a BBBOnline participant will display a privacy seal on the website's homepage or on its privacy statement. The seal provides a link to the validation page of the BBBOnline website. To verify that the website is a member of the BBBOnline seal program, they can view a list of participants on the BBBOnline website (http://us.bbb.org/).

Before filing a complaint with BBBOnline, consumers are asked to review the eligibility criteria posted on their website. Consumers are also advised to make a good faith effort to contact the website operator before filing the complaint. If the consumer cannot reach a satisfactory resolution with the website, they can file the complaint online.

BBBOnline will review the complaint. Consumers are asked to include the following items with their complaint:

1. A copy of all correspondence between the consumer and the organization or company that operates the website.

2. Information for identification purposes.

3. Information about which included materials are confidential and which are not.

BBBOnline will determine the eligibility of the complaint, and evaluate, investigate, analyze, and make a decision about how to resolve the complaint. The complaint will be forwarded to the website for its comments, and will also contact the both parties if it needs additional information.

The website has 15 business days to respond to the complaint. Once the answer is received, it is forwarded to the consumer, who has 10 days to submit any additional information. The reply is then forwarded to the website, which has an additional 10 days to reply. After all information is submitted, a decision will be rendered.

Depending on the nature of the complaint, BBBOnline may require the participating company to change its stated privacy policy or privacy practices. BBBOnline will also have the consumer's information corrected, modified, or deleted, as appropriate. A company that refuses to comply with a BBBOnline decision may be referred to the appropriate government agency, removed from the BBBOnline program, and be subject to legal action with BBBOnline. BBBOnLine also provides an appeals process for matters involving substantial questions or interpretations of BBBOnLine privacy standards, or in situations in which there is a significant possibility that the matter might be decided differently.

Selected provisions of the BBBOnline Code of Online Business Practices can be found in Appendix 11, "Code of Online Business Practices—Selected Provisions," of this Almanac.

INTERNET AUCTIONS

In General

An auction is basically defined as the process of putting merchandise up for a bid and awarding the item to the person who makes the highest bid. An Internet auction is one in which the participants bid for the merchandise online. Unfortunately, the Internet auction presents a number of risks.

According to the Federal Trade Commission (FTC), among the thousands of consumer fraud complaints the FTC receives every year, those dealing with online auction fraud consistently rank near the top of the list. The complaints generally involve problems with shipments and bogus online payment or escrow services. Most complaints involve the seller, but in some cases, the buyer is the subject of the complaint.

The Role of the Internet Auction Website

On most Internet auction sites, individual sellers or small businesses sell their items directly to consumers. In these auctions, the seller has possession of the merchandise and the website does not take responsibility for any problems that may arise between buyers and sellers. Thus before participating, prospective buyers and sellers should read the Internet auction website's terms of use, and review any information the website offers.

Secure Your Registration Information

Most Internet auction sites require buyers and sellers to register and obtain a "user account name" and password before they can make bids or place items for bid. It is important that you keep your registration information private. If you share this information, another person could access your account and buy or sell items without your knowledge. This could damage your online reliability rating as well as your bank account.

Be aware of "phishing" e-mails sent to you, asking for your password or other personal information, that look like they have been sent by an auction website or payment service. Usually, these e-mails are trying to deceive you into providing your personal information, and are coming from someone who wants to hack into your account.

If you get an e-mail or pop-up message that asks for personal or financial information, do not reply or click on the link in the message. Legitimate companies do not ask for this information via e-mail.

If you are concerned about your account, contact the organization mentioned in the e-mail, using a telephone number you know to be genuine, or open a new Internet browser session and type in the company's correct website address yourself. In any case, do not cut and paste the link from the message into your Internet browser. Phishers often make links look like they go to one site, but actually send you somewhere else.

Make Sure Your Transaction is Secure

If you are the successful bidder in an Internet auction, there are a number of ways you can pay for the item, however, you must make sure your payment is secure, and that you are dealing with a legitimate seller. Some sellers limit the method in which payment may be made, however, do not be tricked into providing your credit card or banking information unless the security of the transaction is guaranteed.

Never provide your social security number or driver's license number to a seller. Do not provide your credit card number or bank account information until you have checked out the seller and any online payment service you are asked to use.

Review the privacy statement and security measures disclosed by the online payment service. Never disclose your financial or personal information until you know why it is being collected, how it will be used, and how it will be safeguarded.

Check with the Better Business Bureau, state attorney general or consumer protection agency where you live and where the online payment service is based to see whether there are unresolved complaints against the service. Nevertheless, a lack of complaints does not necessarily mean the service is legitimate.

If the website looks suspicious, e.g., words are misspelled or the quality of the site is inferior, call the customer service line. If there is no customer service number, or they cannot be reached, do not use the service.

Many smaller sellers accept forms of payment that are cash equivalents, such as checks or money orders. You should use this type of payment only when you trust the seller. Unlike credit cards or some online payment services, cash equivalents cannot be reversed if something goes wrong.

In addition, you should not wire transfer money from your bank into the seller's bank account unless you know the seller personally or can verify the seller's identity. If there is a problem with the transaction, you most likely will lose your payment and not have any recourse.

A type of Internet auction fraud involves fake escrow services. The "seller" puts goods up for sale on the Internet auction and insists that the buyer use a particular escrow service. Once the buyer provides the "escrow service" with their payment information, it is sent directly to the so-called seller. The buyer never receives the promised goods, can't locate the seller, and, because the escrow service was part of the scheme, the buyer cannot get any money back.

Avoid doing business with sellers you cannot identify. Some fraudulent sellers use forged e-mail headers that make it impossible to follow up with them if there is a problem. If possible, get the seller's telephone number and dial it to make sure it is legitimate.

It is important to save all transaction information, including the seller's information; the item description; and the time, date and price of your winning bid. Save every e-mail you send to the auction company or seller, and every e-mail you receive from them.

Filing a Complaint

If you suspect an Internet auction transaction is fraudulent, you should file a complaint with the Federal Trade Commission (FTC), as set forth below on its website (www.ftc.gov/). You should also report any fraudulent activity to the Internet auction company.

CONSUMER SENTINEL

Consumer Sentinel is a unique investigative cyber tool provided by the FTC that provides law enforcement members of the Consumer Sentinel Network with access to millions of consumer complaints. Consumer Sentinel includes complaints about: (1) identity theft; (2) do-not-call registry violations; (3) computers, the Internet, and online auctions; (4) telemarketing scams; (5) advance-fee loans and credit scams; (6) sweepstakes, lotteries, and prizes; (7) business opportunities and work-at-home schemes; (8) health and weight loss products; and (9) debt collection, credit reports, and financial matters.

The Consumer Sentinel Network provides law enforcement members with access to complaints provided directly to the Federal Trade Commission by consumers, as well as providing members with access to complaints shared by data contributors, who include: (1) participated

Better Business Bureaus (BBBs); (2) The Internet Crime Complaint Center (IC3); (3) Phonebusters; (4) The U.S. Postal Inspection Service (USPIS); (5) The National Fraud Information Center (NFIC); and (6) The Identity Theft Assistance Center (ITAC).

CROSS-BORDER CONSUMER INTERNET COMPLAINTS

On April 24, 2001, thirteen countries concerned with consumer protection and confidence in e-commerce involving multinational Internet transactions began "econsumer.gov," a joint effort to gather and share cross-border e-commerce complaints.

E-consumer Complaints—Products or Services

E-consumer complaints concerning products or services filed with *econsumer.gov* from January 1 through June 30, 2007 included: shop-at-home/catalogue sales (45%); lotteries (9%); Internet auction (8%); computers/software equipment (7%); foreign money offers (5%); credit cards (3%); cars (3%); work-at-home plans (3%); banks (3%); clothing (3%); prizes/sweepstakes/gifts (3%); and other (8%).

E-consumer Complaints—Violations

E-consumer complaints concerning violations filed with *econsumer.gov* from January 1 through June 30, 2007 included: merchandise or service never received (20%); other misrepresentation (17%); cannot contact merchant (10%); failure to honor refund policy (7%); unauthorized use of identity/account information (6%); billed for unordered merchandise or service (4%); defective/poor quality (4%); undisclosed or unsubstantiated charges (3%); merchandise or service not in conformity with order (3%); failure to honor warranty or guarantee (3%); and other violations (24%).

E-consumer Complaints—Consumer Locations

The top ten consumer locations from which E-consumer complaints were filed with *econsumer.gov* from January 1 through June 30, 2007 were: the United States (5,332); Australia (371); the United Kingdom (213); Canada (191); France (90); Germany (68); India (58); Spain (54); Mexico (43); and Belgium (38).

E-consumer Complaints—Company Locations

The top ten company locations from which E-consumer complaints were filed with *econsumer.gov* from January 1 through June 30, 2007 were: the United Kingdom (1,497); the United States (1,278); Canada (427); China (355); Nigeria (224); Australia (162); Germany (157); Spain (147); Netherlands (133); and Hong Kong (124).

Project Components

The EConsumer.gov project has two components: (1) a multilingual public website; and (2) a government, password-protected website.

Public Website

The public website provides consumers with general information about consumer protection in all countries that belong to the International Consumer Protection Enforcement Network (ICPEN); contact information for consumer protection authorities in those countries; and an online complaint form. All information is available in English, French, German, and Spanish.

Countries that belong to ICPEN include: Australia, Austria, Azerbaijan, Belgium, Canada, Chile, China, Czech Republic, Denmark, Estonia, Finland, France, Germany, Greece, Hungary, Ireland, Italy, Japan, Latvia, Lithuania, Luxembourg, Malta, Mexico, Netherlands, New Zealand, Norway, Poland, Portugal, Slovakia, South Korea, Spain, Sweden, Switzerland, United Kingdom, and the United States of America.

A directory of ICPEN member countries can be found in Appendix 12, "Directory of ICPEN Member Countries," of this Almanac.

Government Website

Using the existing FTC Consumer Sentinel network described above, the incoming complaints will be shared through the government website with participating consumer protection law enforcement agencies.

Filing a Complaint

Your complaint may be entered into Consumer Sentinel. As discussed above, Consumer Sentinel is the consumer complaint database maintained by the FTC. Consumer Sentinel accepts complaints from consumers about online and related transactions with foreign companies.

You can access the online complaint form on the FTC website (https://econsumer.ftccomplaintassistant.gov/). Once entered, your complaint is accessible to certified government law enforcement and regulatory agencies in ICPEN-member countries. In addition, you can access your complaint to update or correct it by contacting the FTC and identifying your complaint by the assigned reference number.

Nevertheless, you should not necessarily expect any country to pursue your complaint on your behalf. Many government agencies bring law enforcement actions to protect the public-at-large, but do not intervene on behalf of individual consumers. Other agencies have an obligation to investigate each complaint.

Whether or not your complaint is investigated on an individual basis, it is important to provide this information to Consumer Sentinel. The Internet marketplace is a borderless one, thus sharing your complaint with government agencies in different countries will help keep the Internet safe. It will also help prevent others from experiencing the problem you did.

Government agencies may use this information to investigate suspect companies and individuals, uncover new scams, and spot trends in fraud. Information submitted through the online complaint form may also be used in aggregate form to analyze trends and statistics that may be released to the public. This joint effort helps to protect all Internet users.

CHAPTER 4:
ONLINE FINANCIAL SERVICES

IN GENERAL

The days of having to get to your bank during "banker's hours" to carry out your financial transactions are over. Most banks have extended weekday hours, and some banks are open 7 days a week. ATM machines are available 24 hours/7 days a week for deposits, cash withdrawals, payments, and other services.

Banking has undergone drastic changes in the last thirty years. Now, you don't even have to leave the comfort of your home to do your banking and carry out other financial transactions. All you need is a computer and access to the Internet. Unfortunately, online banking creates privacy risks and opens up new opportunities for identity thieves. Therefore, it is important to make sure your financial institution has security measures in place that will protect your information.

INTERNET BANKING

Internet banking is a rapidly growing technology available through most banks. In fact, studies have indicated that there is substantial customer demand for these accommodations and banks have to offer this service in order to stay competitive. One of the biggest advantages of Internet banking is the ability to pay your bills online. Another advantage is the ability to bank at any hour of the day, any day of the week, from any location where you have access to a computer and an Internet connection.

Unfortunately, there are also some disadvantages that must be considered when banking online. You have to learn to navigate the bank's online features, and make sure you know which buttons to press to carry out a particular task. In addition, in order to participate in Internet banking, you must necessarily divulge a lot of your personal identifying and financial information, which raises privacy and security concerns.

Protect Your PIN

In order to sign up for Internet banking, you must first access your bank's website and follow the procedure for setting up your online banking account. After providing your account number and other identifying information, you are generally asked to choose a username and a password that you will use to access your existing accounts electronically.

It is important to safeguard your username and password very carefully. Your password is just as valuable as the PIN number assigned to your ATM card. Don't use a password that can easily be guessed by an identity thief, such as your birthday. It is also wise to change your password from time to time to minimize the risk that your account will be accessed. In addition, if you receive an e-mail asking you to confirm your password, do not respond. Your bank will not send you an e-mail asking for this information. Call your bank and report the e-mail request.

Online Activities

Once registered, you can generally view your bank statements online, including recent activity, download your statements to your computer, and view imaged copies of individual items, without having to wait for your statements in the mail. In addition, most banks also offer you the ability to view the long-term activity on your account. You may also be able to link all of your bank and credit card accounts, transfer funds between accounts, open new accounts, apply for loans, order checks, make investments, and pay bills online.

Online Bill Payment

Online bill payment is becoming increasingly popular with consumers. Many banks that offer Internet banking also provide their customers with the ability to pay their bills online using their bank account. The bank generally provides a list of payees, and the customer chooses the payees from that list. If a payee is not listed, the customer must type in the payee's name, address, telephone number, and the customer's account number with the payee. This information is then stored and the customer need only enter the payment amount and date for the particular payee when it is time to pay that bill. The customer can thereafter track the status of bill payments online at any time.

Depending on the payee, the bill will be paid either electronically or by a paper check which is printed and mailed by the bank. An increasing number of companies are now equipped to accept direct electronic payments, which are transmitted instantaneously. Nevertheless, it is still advisable to schedule payments approximately 5 days in advance to make sure the payees receive timely payments and avoid late charges.

The customer can also request automatic bill payment for bills that are paid in the same amount and at the same time each month, such as an installment loan. The bank will automatically make those payments from the customer's account each month. The customer must be careful, however, to notate the monthly deduction in their checking or saving account ledger each month.

Many companies also offer their customers the option of receiving electronic bills (e-bills) instead of mailing a paper bill. The e-bill is transmitted to the customer over the Internet. It contains all of the same information as the paper bill, and offers the customer the opportunity to pay the bill online.

Nevertheless, it is crucial if you are going to take advantage of any of these services that require you to provide a large amount of personal financial and identifying information, that you make sure your connection is secure, as discussed below.

Links to Third Party Websites

As an added convenience to customers, some banks offer online links to merchants, retail stores, travel agents, and other non-financial sites. However, your bank may not guarantee the products and services offered by an outside company even though they provided a link to the website, and will disclaim any liability. In addition, third-party websites may have different privacy policies and/or security standards governing their sites than those provided by your bank. Further, non-financial websites that are linked to your bank's website are not FDIC-insured.

Security Concerns

Unfortunately, identity thieves who are able to obtain your username and password are also able to access this wealth of information and services. Further, if the bank's website is not secure, identity thieves who are knowledgeable computer hackers may be able to access information through the bank's website.

Given the extensive amount of personal identifying and financial information involved in Internet banking, there are serious concerns relating to security issues, thus banks should be very careful in selecting and developing an appropriate software system with a secure online server to process their customer's banking transactions.

You should inquire about the bank's online security procedures to make sure that your information is secure and the risk of interception by identity thieves is minimized. Review your bank's website for information about its security practices, or contact the bank directly.

Most banks use Secure Socket Layer (SSL) technology to encrypt your personal information such as your username, password, and account information over the Internet. Any information provided to you is scrambled en route and decoded once it reaches your browser. In addition, information you provide via electronic forms will be scrambled en route and decoded once it reaches the bank.

You may check that your web session is secure by looking for a small lock symbol usually located in the lower corner of your web browser window. Current versions of leading web browsers indicate when a web page is encrypted for transmission through this symbol. You may also look for the letters "https://" at the beginning of your website URL in your web browser. The "s" means that the web connection is secure.

In addition, e-mail you send within your bank website should be secure, however, e-mail sent though any other means may not be secure unless the bank advises you that security measures will be in place prior to your transmitting the information. Therefore, do not send confidential information such as social security or account numbers to your bank via an unsecured e-mail.

You should also find make sure your computer is secure and operating with all available security features, including anti-virus software. Contact your hardware and software suppliers or Internet service provider to ensure you have the latest in security updates.

Computer security is discussed more fully in Chapter 1, "Securing Your Computer," of this Almanac.

THE GRAMM-LEACH-BLILEY ACT (GLBA)

The Gramm-Leach-Bliley Act (GLBA)—also known as the Financial Services Modernization Act—was signed into law by President Clinton on November 12, 1999. The Act gives consumers certain rights to protect their personal financial information. Safeguarding the personal identifying information of customers is particularly important insofar as so much banking and investment activity is now conducted over the Internet, which can present significant privacy and security challenges.

As discussed below, the Act contains three major sections that govern the collection, disclosure, and protection of a customer's personal information: (1) The Financial Privacy Rule; (2) The Safeguards Rule; and (3) The Pretexting Protection.

Selected provisions of Gramm-Leach-Bliley Act can be found in Appendix 13, "The Gramm-Leach-Bliley Act—Selected Provisions," of this Almanac.

The Financial Privacy Rule

The Financial Privacy Rule of the GLBA (Subtitle A: Disclosure of Nonpublic Personal Information) is codified at 15 U.S.C. § 6801–6809).

The Financial Privacy Rule applies to financial institutions that are under the jurisdiction of the Federal Trade Commission (FTC). This includes non-bank companies that engage in a wide array of financial activities such as:

1. lending, brokering, or servicing any type of consumer loan;

2. transferring or safeguarding money;

3. preparing individual tax returns;

4. providing financial advice or credit counseling;

5. providing residential real estate settlement services;

6. collecting consumer debts; and

7. various other financial activities.

The Financial Privacy Rule is concerned with the protection of the consumer's non-public information. The rule requires financial institutions to give their customers privacy notices that explain the financial institution's information collection and sharing practices. In turn, customers have the right to limit some sharing of their information. Also, financial institutions and other companies that receive personal financial information from a financial institution may be limited in their ability to use that information.

The FTC is one of eight federal agencies that, along with the states, are responsible for developing a consistent regulatory framework to administer and enforce the Financial Privacy Rule. Basically, the Rule requires financial institutions to provide each consumer with a privacy notice at the time the relationship is established, and yearly thereafter.

The required privacy notice must detail the type of information collected, how that information is used and shared, and perhaps most importantly, how that information is protected. In addition, the consumer has a right to "opt out" of the information sharing provision as it pertains to parties who are not affiliated with the financial institution. If the financial institution amends their privacy policy, the consumer must be notified again, and is given the right to opt out again.

The Safeguards Rule

The Safeguards Rule of the GLBA (Subtitle A: Disclosure of Nonpublic Personal Information) is codified at 15 U.S.C. § 6801–6809.

Under the Gramm-Leach-Bliley Act, the Safeguards Rule, enforced by the FTC, requires financial institutions to have a security plan to protect the confidentiality and integrity of personal consumer information.

The Safeguards Rule applies to businesses, regardless of size, that are "significantly engaged" in providing financial products or services to consumers. This includes check-cashing businesses, data processors, mortgage brokers, non-bank lenders, personal property or real estate appraisers, professional tax prepares, courier services, and retailers that issue credit cards to consumers.

The Safeguards Rule also applies to financial companies—such as credit reporting agencies and ATM operators—that receive information from other financial institutions about their customers. In addition to developing their own safeguards, financial institutions are responsible for taking steps to ensure that their affiliates and service providers safeguard customer information in their care. Poorly managed customer data can lead to identity theft which occurs when someone steals a consumer's personal identifying information for illegal purposes, e.g., to fraudulently open new charge accounts, order merchandise, or borrow money.

The Safeguards Rule requires financial institutions to develop a written information security plan that describes their program to protect customer information. The plan must be appropriate to the financial institution's size and complexity, the nature and scope of its activities, and the sensitivity of the customer information it handles.

As part of its security plan, each financial institution must:

1. designate one or more employees to coordinate the safeguards;

2. identify and assess the risks to customer information in each relevant area of the company's operation, and evaluate the effectiveness of the current safeguards for controlling these risks;

3. design and implement a "safeguards" program, and regularly monitor and test it;

4. select appropriate service providers and contract with them to implement safeguards; and

5. evaluate and adjust the program in light of relevant circumstances, including changes in the firm's business arrangements or operations, or the results of testing and monitoring of safeguards.

Each financial institution is advised to implement safeguards appropriate to its own circumstances. For example, some financial institutions may choose to describe their safeguards programs in a single document, while others may set forth their plans in several different documents, such as one to cover an information technology division and another to describe the training program for employees.

Similarly, a company may decide to designate a single employee to coordinate safeguards or may spread this responsibility among several employees who will work together.

In addition, a firm with a small staff may design and implement a more limited employee training program than a firm with a large number of employees. A financial institution that doesn't receive or store any information online may take fewer steps to assess risks to its computers than a firm that routinely conducts its business online.

When a firm implements safeguards, the Safeguards Rule requires it to consider all areas of its operation. As discussed below, the following three areas are particularly important to information security: (1) Employee Management and Training; (2) Information Systems; and (3) Managing System Failures.

Employee Management and Training

The success or failure of a company's information security plan depends largely on the employees who implement it. Therefore, the company must carefully check the references of all potential employees who will have access to customer information. In addition, new employees should be required to sign an agreement acknowledging their responsibility for following the company's confidentiality and security standards for handling customer information. Further, access to customer information should be limited to employees who have a business reason to have the information.

Employees should be properly trained in maintaining the security, confidentiality and integrity of customer information. The FTC advises businesses to take the following steps to ensure the security of customer information:

1. maintain locking rooms and file cabinets where paper records are kept;

2. use password-activated screensavers;

3. use strong passwords that are at least eight characters long;

4. change passwords periodically, and do not post passwords near employees' computers;

5. encrypt sensitive customer information when it is transmitted electronically over networks or stored online;

6. refer calls or other requests for customer information to designated individuals who have had safeguards training; and

7. recognize any fraudulent attempt to obtain customer information and report it to appropriate law enforcement agencies.

Information Systems

Information systems include network and software design, and information processing, storage, transmission, retrieval, and disposal. Security should be maintained throughout the life cycle of customer information—i.e., from data entry to data disposal. The FTC advises businesses to take the following steps to ensure that customer information remains secure:

Storage of Information

1. paper records should be stored in a secure area that can only be accessed by authorized employees;

2. electronic customer information should be stored on a secure server that is accessible only with a password or other security protection;

3. sensitive customer data should not be stored on a machine with an Internet connection; and

4. backup files should be securely maintained, e.g., by storing off-line or in a physically secure area.

Retrieval and Transmission of Information

When collecting or transmitting customer information, data transmission should be secure. For example:

1. When collecting credit card information or other sensitive financial data, a Secure Sockets Layer (SSL) or other secure connection should be used so that the information is encrypted in transit.

2. When collecting information directly from consumers, secure transmission should be automatic and customers should be cautioned against transmitting sensitive data, such as their account numbers, by e-mail; and

3. When transmitting sensitive data by e-mail, make sure the messages are password protected so that only authorized employees have access to the information.

Disposal of Information

Customer information should be disposed of in a secure manner. For example:

1. a records retention manager should be designated to supervise the disposal of records containing nonpublic personal information;

2. customer information recorded on paper should be shredded or recycled and stored in a secure area until picked up by a recycling service;

3. when disposing of computers, diskettes, magnetic tapes, hard drives or any other electronic media, all data that contains customer information should be erased;

4. hardware should be effectively destroyed; and

5. outdated customer information should be disposed of promptly.

Managing System Failures

Effective security management includes the prevention, detection and response to attacks, intrusions or other system failures. The FTC advises businesses to take the following steps to effectively manage their information systems:

1. maintain and follow a written contingency plan to address any breaches of physical, administrative or technical safeguards;

2. check with software vendors regularly to obtain and install patches that resolve software vulnerabilities;

3. use anti-virus software that updates automatically;

4. maintain up-to-date firewalls, particularly if the business uses broadband Internet access or allows employees to connect to the computer network from home or at other off-site locations;

5. provide central management of security tools for employees and pass along updates about any security risks or breaches;

6. take steps to preserve the security, confidentiality and integrity of customer information in the event of a computer or other technological failure, e.g., back up all customer data regularly;

7. maintain systems and procedures to ensure that access to nonpublic consumer information is granted only to legitimate and

valid users, e.g., by using passwords combined with personal identifiers to authenticate the identity of customers; and

8. notify customers promptly if their nonpublic personal information is subject to loss, damage or unauthorized access.

The Pretexting Protection

The Pretexting Provision of the GLBA (Subtitle B: Fraudulent Access to Financial Information) is codified at 15 U.S.C. § 6821–6827).

The Gramm-Leach-Bliley Act prohibits "pretexting"—the use of false pretenses, including fraudulent statements and impersonation—to obtain another's personal financial information. The pretexter first gains access to the consumer's private information, such as their social security number or date of birth. The pretexter then uses this information to trick a company into disclosing even more private information about the victim, such as bank balances, credit lines, tax information, etc.

The law also prohibits the knowing solicitation of others to engage in pretexting. The FTC actively initiates lawsuits to stop companies and individuals who practice pretexting and selling consumers' financial information.

FILING A COMPLAINT

If you think a financial institution or company has failed to fulfill its responsibilities under the law, you file a complaint with the federal agency listed below that has enforcement jurisdiction over that financial institution or company.

State Member Banks of the Federal Reserve System

Consumer and Community Affairs
Board of Governors of the Federal Reserve System
20th & C Streets, NW, Mail Stop 801
Washington, DC 20551
Website: http://www.federalreserve.gov/

National Banks

Office of the Comptroller of the Currency
Compliance Management
Mail Stop 7–5
Washington, DC 20219
Website: http://www.occ.treas.gov/

Federal Credit Unions

National Credit Union Administration
1775 Duke Street
Alexandria, VA 22314
Website: http://www.ncua.gov/

Non-Member Federally Insured Banks

Office of Consumer Programs
Federal Deposit Insurance Corporation
550 17th Street, NW
Washington, DC 20429
Website: http://www.fdic.gov/

Federally Insured Savings and Loans, and Federally Chartered State Banks

Consumer Affairs Program
Office of Thrift Supervision
1700 G Street, NW
Washington, DC 20552
Website: http://www.ots.treas.gov/

CHAPTER 5:
PROTECTING CHILDREN'S PRIVACY
ONLINE

IN GENERAL

Children encompass one of the largest groups of Internet users. Children use the Internet to access a wealth of information to help them with their schoolwork, as well as for entertainment and communication purposes, such as gaming, downloading music, and socializing. According to a recent survey, 26% of children spend up to two hours online on a typical day.

The Internet provides many educational advantages for children that earlier generations could not have imagined. However, along with these benefits, there are serious concerns about online privacy and safety for children. Although children learn how to use the Internet at a very early age—often as young as 6 years old—they still lack maturity and judgment, which may lead them to divulge personal information that should not be revealed.

PROTECTING YOUR CHILD'S PERSONAL INFORMATION

In General

When a child registers on a website, the website often requests that the child provide personal information, such as their name, address, e-mail address, preferences about products, favorite activities, etc. The information collected may be used in other areas of the website, such as member profiles and chat rooms. The information may also be used to create a customer list. Customer lists are often sold to brokers, who may then sell the list to an advertiser.

When a child's personal information is disseminated, it may enable others to contact the child. There have been a number of cases where children have been contacted online by child predators who try and gain the child's confidence and have bad intentions. Some of these online conversations have led to personal contact, sexual molestation, and murder.

Therefore, parents are advised to oversee their children's online activities, including the websites they visit and the individuals with whom they communicate. The importance of privacy online should be emphasized and they should be advised not to give out their name and address when communicating in chat rooms or on message boards.

In addition, it is crucial for parents to require their children to obtain permission before giving out personal information online, including their name, address or any other information about them or their family. If you become aware of a website that is collecting information from children without requiring parental consent, an online complaint may be made to the Federal Trade Commission (FTC) on their website (kidsprivacy@ftc.gov).

Website Privacy Statements

It is important to read the privacy statement of any website your child may visit in order to determine exactly how the child's personal information may be used. The privacy statement explains how the website uses the information collected from its visitors. If a website does not have a privacy policy, it is best not to patronize that website. As further explained in Chapter 3, "E-commerce," of this Almanac, the privacy statement is a legally binding document.

Parents and children should read the privacy statement together and the child should be taught the meaning of its content. The privacy statement of any website that is linked should also be reviewed. The privacy statement should explain how a parent can review, change or delete any information that the website has collected from their child.

The TRUSTe Children's Privacy Seal

As set forth in Chapter 3, "E-commerce," TRUSTe is a nonprofit third-party oversight program that regularly monitors the adherence of websites to their privacy statements. TRUSTe has the power to enforce compliance with its program.

The TRUSTEe Children's Privacy Seal is a trustmark awarded only to websites that adhere to established privacy principles of disclosure, choice, access and security. The TRUSTEe Children's Privacy seal means that the particular website is dedicated to protecting a child's online privacy, and that the user has the ability to control how their personal information is used by that website.

The TRUSTe Children's Privacy Seal is a seal for websites that are directed at children under 13. Every website displaying the TRUSTe Children's Seal must:

1. Adhere to the privacy principles of notice, choice, access, and security;

2. Obtain verifiable parental consent before collecting personally identifiable information from a child; and

3. Allow a parent to access and delete a child's personal information at any time.

The TRUSTe Children's Seal on a website also means that the site can be trusted to abide by the guarantees it gives in its privacy statement. Generally, the privacy statement can be accessed by clicking on the privacy seal.

If a parent believes their child's privacy has been violated on a website displaying the TRUSTe Children's Seal, they are advised to contact TRUSTe directly by registering a complaint on their website (www. truste.org/users/users_watchdog.html).

PARENTAL CONTROLS

Since it is impossible to constantly monitor a child's online activity, it is important to make sure your child cannot visit sites that are unsuitable for children. Most major Internet Service Providers provide parental controls that allow you to adjust the nature of content available to each screen name. Parental controls allow you to place restrictions on the websites a child is allowed to access and the amount of unsolicited e-mail a child may receive. This means each family member can have customized access to the Internet based on age at no additional charge.

For example, America Online has four age categories for which parental controls may be set:

Kids (12 & Under)

This category, if selected, provides the following protections:

1. blocks content and services inappropriate for kids, and filters searches for age-appropriate material;

2. restricts children to child-friendly websites;

3. blocks e-mails with attachments, pictures and hyper links;

4. restricts instant messages to approved contacts only;

5. blocks instant messages with files, images, voice, and video;

6. provides for 100% monitored chats only and blocks hyperlinks;

7. controls the amount of time the child spends online, if this feature is activated; and

8. provides a report of the child's online activity, if this feature is activated.

Young Teens (13–15)

This category, if selected, provides the following protections:

1. blocks content and services inappropriate for young teens, and filters searches for age-appropriate material;

2. blocks websites with adult, violent, or mature content;

3. blocks e-mails with attachments, pictures, and hyper links;

4. blocks instant messages with files, images, voice, and video;

5. blocks access to certain AOL chatrooms and hyperlinks.

6. controls the amount of time the child spends online, if this feature is activated; and

7. provides a report of the child's online activity, if this feature is activated.

Mature Teens (16–17)

This category, if selected, provides the following protections:

1. blocks content and services inappropriate for mature teens, and filters searches for age-appropriate material;

2. blocks websites with adult or violent content;

3. blocks access to certain AOL chatrooms and hyperlinks;

4. controls the amount of time the child spends online, if this feature is activated; and

5. provides a report of the child's online activity, if this feature is activated.

THE CHILDREN'S ONLINE PRIVACY PROTECTION ACT OF 1998 (COPPA)

Several years ago, a number of websites were encouraging children to provide personal information about themselves or their family for their own marketing purposes. Some of these websites enticed children with games and free gifts. In response to this kind of activity, Congress passed the Children's Online Privacy Protection Act of 1998 (COPPA).

COPPA Not COPA

COPPA should not be confused with the Child Online Protection Act of 1998 (COPA). The statutes were enacted in the same year and have nearly identical titles. COPA was concerned with preventing a child's from accessing age-inappropriate websites. COPA required all *commercial* distributors of *material harmful to minors* to protect their websites from access by minors, defined as children under the age of 17.

In July 2008, the U.S. Court of Appeals for the Third Circuit found that COPA was unconstitutionally broad and vague, and not tailored to advance the government's interest in protecting children. The Court also found that the provisions in COPA suppressed a large part of speech that adults have a constitutional right to receive.

The COPPA Rule

The implementing rules for the Act promulgated by the Federal Trade Commission (FTC) took effect April 21, 2000. The primary goal of the COPPA Rule is to give parents control over what information is collected from their children online and how such information may be used.

The COPPA Rule applies to individually identifiable information about a child such as name, home address, e-mail address, telephone number or any other information that would allow someone to identify or contact the child. The Rule also covers other types of information, such as hobbies, interests, and information collected through cookies or other types of tracking mechanisms when they are tied to individually identifiable information.

Covered Website Operators

The COPPA Rule applies to:

1. operators of commercial websites and online services directed to children under 13 that collect personal information from them;

2. operators of general audience websites that knowingly collect personal information from children under 13; and

3. operators of general audience websites that have a separate children's area and that collect personal information from children under 13.

The COPPA Rule sets out a number of factors in determining whether a website is targeted to children, such as the website's: (1) subject matter;

(2) language; (3) whether it uses animated characters; and (4) whether advertising appearing on the site is directed to children.

The FTC will also consider empirical evidence regarding the ages of the site's visitors. These standards are very similar to those previously established for TV, radio, and print advertising.

Foreign-Based Website Operators

The definition of "website operator" under both COPPA and the COPPA Rule includes foreign-based websites that are involved in commerce in the United States or its territories.

Foreign-based websites must comply with COPPA and the COPPA Rule if they are directed to children in the United States, or if they knowingly collect personal information from children in the United States.

As a related matter, U.S.-based websites that collect information from foreign children also are subject to COPPA and the COPPA Rule.

Notification Requirements

Under the COPPA Rule, the website operator must post a link to a notice of its information practices on the home page of its website or online service and at each area where it collects personal information from children. An operator of a general audience site with a separate children's area must post a link to its notice on the home page of the children's area.

The link to the privacy notice must be clear and prominent. The notice must be clearly written and understandable. It should not include any unrelated or confusing materials. It must state the following information:

1. The name and contact information, including address, telephone number and e-mail address, of all operators collecting or maintaining children's personal information through the website or online service. If more than one operator is collecting information at the site, the site may select and provide contact information for only one operator who will respond to all inquiries from parents about the site's privacy policies. However, the names of all operators must be listed in the notice.

2. The kinds of personal information collected from children and how the information is collected—e.g., directly from the child, or passively, for example, through cookies.

3. How the operator uses the personal information.

4. Whether the operator discloses information collected from children to third parties. If so, the operator also must disclose the kinds of

businesses in which the third parties are engaged; the general purposes for which the information is used; and whether the third parties have agreed to maintain the confidentiality and security of the information.

5. That the parent has the option to agree to the collection and use of the child's information without consenting to the disclosure of the information to third parties.

6. That the operator may not require a child to disclose more information than is reasonably necessary to participate in an activity as a condition of participation.

7. That the parent can review the child's personal information, ask to have it deleted, and refuse to allow any further collection or use of the child's information. The notice also must state the procedures for the parent to follow.

Verifiable Parental Consent

Before collecting, using or disclosing personal information from a child, the website operator must obtain verifiable parental consent from the child's parent. This means the website operator must make reasonable efforts to ensure that before personal information is collected from a child, a parent of the child receives notice of the website operator's information practices and consents to those practices.

The notice to parents must contain the same information included in the notice on the website, must be written clearly and understandably, and must not contain any unrelated or confusing information.

The notice must state: (1) that it wishes to collect personal information from the child; (2) that the parent's consent is required for the collection, use and disclosure of the information; and (3) how the parent can provide consent.

The website operator must give a parent the option to agree to the collection and use of the child's personal information without agreeing to the disclosure of the information to third parties. However, when a parent agrees to the collection and use of their child's personal information, the website operator may release that information to others who use it solely to provide support for the internal operations of the website or service, including technical support and order fulfillment.

Method of Notification

The website operator may use any one of a number of methods to notify a parent, including sending an e-mail message to the parent or a notice by postal mail.

Website operators may use e-mail to get parental consent for all internal uses of personal information, such as marketing back to a child based on his or her preferences or communicating promotional updates about site content, as long as they take additional steps to increase the likelihood that the parent has, in fact, provided the consent.

The website operator is required to send a new notice and request for consent to parents if there are material changes in the collection, use or disclosure practices to which the parent had previously agreed.

Verification of Parental Identity

Website operators must use reasonable procedures to ensure they are dealing with the child's parent before they provide access to the child's specific information. They can use a variety of methods to verify the parent's identity. For example, the website operator may:

1. obtain a signed form from the parent via postal mail or facsimile;

2. accept and verify a credit card number;

3. take calls from parents on a toll-free telephone number staffed by trained personnel;

4. accept an e-mail from the parent accompanied by digital signature;

5. accept an e-mail from the parent accompanied by a PIN or password obtained through one of the verification methods above.

Operators who follow one of these procedures acting in good faith to a request for parental access are protected from liability under federal and state law for inadvertent disclosures of a child's information to someone who purports to be a parent.

Revocation of Consent

At any time, a parent may: (1) revoke his or her consent; (2) refuse to allow the website operator to further use or collect their child's personal information; and (3) direct the website operator to delete the child's information.

In turn, the website operator may terminate any service provided to the child, but only if the child's personal information—such as the child's e-mail address—is reasonably necessary for the child's participation in that activity. If other activities on the website do not require the child's personal information, the operator must allow the child access to those activities.

Exceptions

The Rule includes several exceptions that allow website operators to collect a child's e-mail address without getting the parent's consent in advance. These exceptions cover many popular online activities for children, including contests, online newsletters, homework help, and electronic postcards.

Thus prior parental consent is not required when:

1. the website operator collects a child's or parent's e-mail address to provide notice and seek consent;

2. the website operator collects an e-mail address to respond to a one-time request from a child and then deletes it;

3. the website operator collects an e-mail address to respond more than once to a specific request, in which case the operator must notify the parent that it is communicating regularly with the child and give the parent the opportunity to stop the communication before sending or delivering a second communication to a child;

4. the website operator collects a child's name or online contact information to protect the safety of a child who is participating on the site, in which case the operator must notify the parent and give him or her the opportunity to prevent further use of the information;

5. the website operator collects a child's name or online contact information to protect the security or liability of the site or to respond to law enforcement, if necessary, and does not use it for any other purpose.

Teen Websites

As discussed above, the COPPA Rule applies to websites that are directed to children under the age of 13. However, many websites intended for teenagers also attract a substantial number of younger children. The COPPA Rule applies to teen and general audience websites if the website operator has actual knowledge that a particular visitor is a child. If a website knows that a particular visitor is a child, then the COPPA Rule must be followed with respect to that child.

A teen website is advised to "age-screen" in a manner that does not invite falsification. If reasonable measures are taken to screen for age, then the website operator is not responsible if a child misstates his or her age.

For example, the website should request age information in a neutral manner at the point where visitors are asked to provide personal information or to create their log-in user ID. In designing a neutral age-screening mechanism, a website operator can implement a system that allows a user to freely enter month, day, and year of birth.

A website that includes a drop-down menu that only permits users to enter birth years making them 13 or older, would not be considered a neutral age-screening mechanism since children cannot enter their correct age on that site. In addition, a site that does not ask for neutral date of birth information but rather simply includes a check box stating "I am over 12 years old" would not be considered a neutral age-screening mechanism.

In addition, the website should employ temporary or permanent "cookies" to prevent younger children from back-buttoning to change their age in order to circumvent the parental consent requirement or to obtain access to the website.

However, once a child under age 13 is identified, the website operator has two options:

1. collect the parents' e-mail address to provide direct notice and implement COPPA's parental consent requirements; or,

2. if you do not wish to implement the COPPA protections for visitors under age 13, configure the website's data system to automatically delete the personal information of those visitors under 13 and direct them to content, if available, that does not involve collection or disclosure of personal information.

If the website operator ask participants to enter age information, and then fails to either screen out or obtain parental consent from those users who indicate that they are under 13, the website operator may be liable for violating COPPA and the COPPA Rule.

Nevertheless, if the website falls into one of the exceptions described above, prior parental consent may not be required.

Compliance and Enforcement

The FTC monitors the Internet for compliance with the COPPA Rule and brings law enforcement actions where appropriate to deter violations. The FTC has obtained numerous federal district court settlements against website operators who are alleged to have violated the COPPA Rule.

A court can hold website operators who violate the COPPA Rule liable for civil penalties of up to $11,000 per violation. The amount of penalties the court assesses may turn on a number of factors, including: (1) the egregiousness of the violation; (2) the number of children involved; (3) the amount and type of personal information collected; (4) how the information was used; (5) whether the information was shared with third parties; and (6) the size of the company.

The FTC has set up a special webpage designed for children, parents, businesses, and educators (http://www.ftc.gov/kidzprivacy). In addition to providing compliance materials for businesses and parents, this webpage features online safety tips for children and other useful educational resources about COPPA and related rules and online privacy in general.

Filing a Complaint

Parents and others can submit complaints to the FTC for violations of the COPPA Rule. Consumer groups, industry members, FTC-approved COPPA safe harbor programs, and other members of the public also may provide information concerning website operators that may not be in compliance with the COPPA Rule.

In order to file a complaint, you may call the FTC toll free telephone number, (877) FTC-HELP, to submit your complaint to a live operator. The FTC website also has an online form to file complaints or request information, accessible through the "File a Complaint" link at the top of the website's homepage (http://www.ftc.gov).

The Safe Harbor Program

In order to encourage active industry self-regulation, COPPA also includes a "safe harbor" provision allowing industry groups and others to request FTC approval of self-regulatory guidelines to govern participating websites' compliance with the COPPA Rule.

The organization must submit its guidelines to the FTC for approval. The FTC will publish submissions for public comment and then make a determination as to whether the guidelines meet the criteria set forth in the COPPA Rule.

The key criteria are that the guidelines: (1) provide the same or greater protections for children as the COPPA Rule; (2) provide effective, mandatory mechanisms for assessing participants' compliance with the requirements; and (3) offer compliance incentives that provide for effective enforcement of the COPPA Rule.

COPPA requires the FTC to act on a request for "safe harbor" treatment within 180 days of the filing of the request. The COPPA Rule sets out the criteria for approval of guidelines and the materials that must be submitted as part of a safe harbor application.

The text of the Children's Online Privacy Protection Act (COPPA) can be found in Appendix 14, "The Children's Online Privacy Protection Act," of this Almanac.

THE CHILDREN'S INTERNET PROTECTION ACT OF 2000 (CIPA)

In General

In 2000, Congress passed the Children's Internet Protection Act (CIPA), a law intended to protect children from accessing material on the Internet that is deemed "harmful to minors." CIPA requires that schools and public libraries use filtering software on all public computers to control the content of material available on a particular computer.

For purposes of CIPA, filtering software is intended to: (1) prevent computer users from viewing images that are obscene or depict child pornography; (2) limit the websites children have access; and (3) restrict content deemed harmful to minors.

Internet Safety Policy

Under CIPA, schools and public libraries must certify that they have an Internet safety policy and technology protection measures in place. The Internet safety policy must include technology protection measures to block or filter Internet access to pictures that are: (1) obscene; (2) child pornography; or (3) harmful to minors.

Schools and libraries subject to CIPA must also certify that, as part of their Internet safety policy, they are educating minors about appropriate online behavior. This includes "cyberbullying" awareness and response, and interaction with other individuals on social networking sites and in chat rooms. In addition, schools are required to adopt and enforce a policy to monitor online activities of minors.

Neighborhood Children's Internet Protection Act

Section 1732 of CIPA sets forth additional Internet safety policy requirements for schools and libraries that address children's use of the Internet. Schools and libraries subject to CIPA must adopt and implement a policy addressing the following:

1. access by minors to inappropriate matter on the Internet;

2. the safety and security of minors when using electronic mail, chat rooms, and other forms of direct electronic communications;

3. unauthorized access, including so-called "hacking," and other unlawful activities by minors online;

4. unauthorized disclosure, use, and dissemination of personal information regarding minors; and

5. restricting minors' access to materials harmful to them.

Selected provisions of the Children's Internet Protection Act can be found in Appendix 15, "Children's Internet Protection Act—Selected Provisions," of this Almanac.

CHAPTER 6:
SOCIALIZING ON THE INTERNET

SOCIAL NETWORKING

Online social networks are websites where people can connect with others who share their interests. An individual can create their own profile and post content on that profile, such as photographs, music, videos and personal information. They can then connect their profile to other individuals ("friends") within the network.

MySpace and *Facebook* are two of the most popular social networking sites. Unfortunately, as discussed below, social networking sites have led to a number of safety and privacy concerns that the industry is continually trying to address through implementation of various online safety tools.

MySpace

MySpace began as a "for profit" free-access social networking site available to the general public over the age of 13. It operates on revenue received through advertising. MySpace ran into problems when a design flaw led to viruses, spam and phishing problems. In addition, reports of privacy and safety issues surfaced, which led to the implementation of stricter privacy policies and safety guidelines.

For example, in 2007, MySpace discovered and deleted 29,000 profiles belonging to registered sex offenders. Unfortunately, a sexual predator intent on "networking" will always find ways to get back in the system, e.g., by providing a fake profile. In addition, there have been reports of teenage girls who arranged to meet men that they had contact with through MySpace, only to end up victims of sexual assault.

Facebook

Facebook began as a social networking site exclusively directed towards college students, and later expanded its user base to include high school students. Facebook has since opened its free-access website to the general public over the age of 13, and boasts more than 120 million users worldwide. Like MySpace, Facebook generates income from advertising.

Facebook has also run into safety and privacy problems. Users are led to believe that personal details on their profile are private. However, savvy computer users demonstrated their ability to write programs that masquerade as games or quizzes while at the same time the application is collecting the user's personal details. When a user adds the application to their profile, their personal information is being harvested, exposing them to potential identity theft.

Joint Statement on Principles of Social Networking Sites Safety

Social networking has raised a lot of concern over privacy and safety issues, particularly as it relates to minors. In January 2008, MySpace and the state Attorneys General for 49 states and the District of Columbia issued a document called the *Joint Statement on Principles of Social Networking Sites Safety* to address safety issues involving MySpace and similar social networks. The Principles were designed for industry-wide adoption, and relate to online safety tools, technology, education, and enforcement cooperation.

Privacy and safety tools implemented as a result of this joint effort include the following:

1. All users may set their profile to private.

2. All users can pre-approve all comments before being posted.

3. Users can block another user from contacting them.

4. Users can conceal their "online now" status.

5. Users can prevent forwarding of their images to other sites.

6. MySpace adds "Report Abuse" button to E-mail, Video, and Forums.

7. Users over 18 can block under 18 users from contacting them or viewing their profiles.

8. All users can allow only those users whom they have proactively added to their contact list to see when they are on IM (instant messaging) and to contact them.

9. Safety Tips available on every page of MySpace.

10. Safety Tips appear on registration page for anyone under 18.

11. Users under 18 must affirmatively consent that user has reviewed the Safety Tips prior to registration. MySpace will require under 18 members to scroll through the complete Safety Tips upon registration. MySpace will also require under 18 members to review the Safety Tips on an annual basis.

12. Additional warning posted to users under 18 regarding disclosure of personal information upon registration.

13. Safety Tips are posted in the "mail" area of all existing users under 18.

14. Safety Tips contain resources for Internet Safety including FTC Tips.

15. Phishing warning added to Safety Tips.

16. Safety tips for parents provides links to free blocking software.

17. Parent able to remove child's profile through the ParentCare Hotline and ParentCare E-mail.

18. MySpace will have "Tom" ("MySpace" founder) become a messenger to deliver Safety Tips to minors on MySpace.

19. All users under 18 receive security warnings before posting content.

MySpace has agreed to continue their research and development of online safety tools, based on recommendations received from the state Attorneys General and online safety advocates. For example, MySpace is organizing an industry-wide Internet Safety Technical Task Force that will explore all new technologies that can help make users more safe and secure.

In addition, MySpace's cooperation with law enforcement, which includes a 24-hour hotline, is viewed as a model for the social networking industry, which enhances the ability of law enforcement officials to investigate and prosecute Internet crimes.

FTC Social Networking Safety Tips

People who subscribe to social networking sites can communicate within a limited community, or with the world at large. The number of "friends" you can invite to view your profile and share information with is virtually unlimited.

Unfortunately, some of these individuals could be dangerous. There have been numerous reports of people who were stalked by someone they met online, had their identity stolen, or had their computer hacked.

Minors are particularly at risk due to their inexperience and generally trusting nature.

The Federal Trade Commission has compiled a set of social networking safety tips designed to make online social networking safer and minimize the risk of identity theft, as set forth below:

1. Think about how different sites work before deciding to join a site. Some sites will allow only a defined community of users to access posted content; others allow anyone and everyone to view postings.

2. Think about keeping some control over the information you post. Consider restricting access to your page to a select group of people, for example, your friends from school, your club, your team, your community groups, or your family.

3. Keep your information to yourself. Don't post your full name, social security number, address, phone number, or bank and credit card account numbers, and don't post other people's information, either. Be cautious about posting information that could be used to identify you or locate you offline. This could include the name of your school, sports team, clubs, and where you work or hang out.

4. Make sure your screen name doesn't say too much about you. Don't use your name, your age, or your hometown. Even if you think your screen name makes you anonymous, it doesn't take a genius to combine clues to figure out who you are and where you can be found.

5. Post only information that you are comfortable with others seeing and knowing about you. Many people can see your page, including your parents, your teachers, the police, the college you might want to apply to next year, or the job you might want to apply for in five years.

6. Remember that once you post information online, you can't take it back. Even if you delete the information from a site, older versions exist on other people's computers.

7. Consider not posting your photo. It can be altered and broadcast in ways you may not be happy about. If you do post one, ask yourself whether it's one your mom would display in the living room.

8. Flirting with strangers online could have serious consequences. Because some people lie about who they really are, you never really know who you're dealing with.

9. Be wary if a new online friend wants to meet you in person. Before you decide to meet someone, do your research. Ask whether any of

your friends know the person, and see what background you can dig up through online search engines. If you decide to meet them, be smart about it. Meet in a public place, during the day, with friends you trust. Tell an adult or a responsible sibling where you're going, and when you expect to be back.

10. Trust your gut if you have suspicions. If you feel threatened by someone or uncomfortable because of something online, tell an adult you trust and report it to the police and the social networking site. You could end up preventing someone else from becoming a victim.

INTERNET DATING

In General

The Internet has introduced a whole new way of finding a mate. Individuals interested in developing a romantic relationship can now do so through the use of a computer in the comfort of their own home. True.com, Match.com and eHarmony are three well-known and popular Internet dating services.

As with most Internet websites, online dating services require the applicant to provide personal information in order to register with the service. This includes information such as age, gender, marital status, location, interests, etc. There are also dating services that cater to more specific criteria, such as race, nationality, religion, and lifestyle. You may also upload a photo to the website, and chat online with potential prospects, both with or without a webcam.

Background Checks

Unfortunately, predators frequent online dating websites looking for potential victims to target for identity theft as well as more heinous crimes, such as stalking and sexual molestation. Thus it is important to find out whether the particular service conducts background checks on subscribers to minimize this risk.

In January 2008, New Jersey became the first state to enact a law requiring the online dating services to disclose whether criminal background checks have been conducted. Other states are considering similar legislation. However, the law has its critics. They claim that the type of screening required by the law—checking for a particular name in databases of criminal convictions—has inherent flaws.

For example, users may give fake names, and many dangerous people may not be in the databases. Employing stricter methods of background checking, such as performing fingerprint scans and researching employment records or social security numbers, is not required under the law.

Virtual Dating

Unlike online dating, individuals who engage in virtual dating do not necessarily intend to meet in person. They use graphic images, called "avatars," to interact in a cybersociety over the Internet without ever leaving their homes. The avatars meet in the virtual world and engage in many activities that physical people would engage in when dating in the real world. For example, the avatars can go out dancing in a nightclub, or have dinner in a fancy restaurant.

The cybersociety represents a real life dating environment. However, virtual dating is not without its safety risks. You don't really know who the person is that you are "dating." It could be a potential stalker, sex offender, identity thief, etc. As you become more and more comfortable with your "virtual" mate, you may accidentally divulge information that could lead to your identity being stolen, or you may even be risking your physical safety.

In order to minimize your risk of becoming a victim, you should not use your real name when creating your avatar profile. Always use an alias when living in your "cybersociety," when chatting, and when sending e-mails. Do not use your primary e-mail. Create a separate e-mail account to use exclusively for your virtual world.

Do not divulge your location or your telephone number. If you do decide to call your virtual mate, block your number before calling in case the conversation becomes suspicious or uncomfortable. If you decide to meet, always do so in a public place and make sure a family member or friend is aware of the meeting.

Until you are completely satisfied and comfortable that the individual has no ulterior motives and does not present a risk to your safety, do not provide any information that will allow him or her to be able to locate you once you have ceased contact.

The International Marriage Broker Regulation Act

In March 2007, the International Marriage Broker Regulation Act (IMBRA) took effect. IMBRA places certain restrictions on internationally oriented dating services that match U.S. clients with potential foreign spouses.

Basically, the law is designed to protect foreign women from sex offenders and abusers by providing the foreign client with information on U.S. laws concerning, among other things, domestic violence, sexual assault, stalking, and involuntary servitude. In addition, the law prohibits such services from providing any personal contact or other information to a U.S. customer about any individual under the age of 18.

In enacting this law, Congress found that this industry has grown significantly in recent years, in large part, facilitated by the Internet. They cited studies that show as many as 500 such companies currently operate in the United States, and it is currently estimated that at least 8,000 to 12,000 individuals in the United States find foreign spouses through for-profit international marriage brokers each year.

Under IMBRA, an internationally oriented dating service may not provide any U.S client with the personal contact information of any foreign national client unless and until the broker has:

1. collected certain background information from the U.S. client to whom the personal contact information would be provided;

2. provided a copy of that background information to the foreign national client in the primary language of that client;

3. provided the foreign national client certain information about legal rights and resources available to immigrant victims of domestic violence and other crimes in the United States;

4. received from the foreign national client, in their primary language, a signed, written consent to release such personal contact information to the specific U.S. client;

5. informed the U.S. client that, after filing a petition for a K nonimmigrant visa, the U.S. client will be subject to a criminal background check.

The background information collected from the U.S. client must be in writing and signed, and may be submitted in electronic form with an electronic signature. It must include information about each of the following:

1. any court order restricting the U.S. client's physical or other contact with, behavior towards, or communication with another person, including any temporary or permanent civil restraining order or protection order;

2. any arrest or conviction of the U.S. client for homicide, murder, manslaughter, assault, battery, domestic violence, rape, sexual assault, abusive sexual contact, sexual exploitation, incest, child abuse or neglect, torture, trafficking, peonage, holding hostage, involuntary servitude, slave trade, kidnapping, abduction, unlawful

criminal restraint, false imprisonment, stalking, or any similar activity in violation of federal, state, or local criminal law;

3. any arrest or conviction of the client for solely, principally, or incidentally engaging in prostitution; or for any direct or indirect attempts to procure prostitutes or persons for the purpose of prostitution; or any receiving, in whole or in part, of the proceeds of prostitution;

4. any arrest or conviction of the client for offenses related to controlled substances or alcohol;

5. marital history of the client including whether the client is currently married; whether the client has previously been married and how many times, how previous marriages of the client were terminated and the date of termination; and if the client has previously sponsored an alien to whom the client or person was engaged or married;

6. the ages of any of the client's children under the age of 18; and

7. all states in which the client or person has resided since the age of 18.

Violations of the Act carry federal penalties of not less than $20,000 and/or imprisonment for each violation. In addition, individual states are entitled to bring a civil action on behalf of the state in a Federal District Court to enforce compliance with the Act.

CHAPTER 7:
INTERNET IDENTITY THEFT

IN GENERAL

Identity theft is a crime that occurs when someone wrongfully obtains and uses another individual's personal information in some way that involves fraud or deception, typically for financial gain. One may first become aware that they are the victim of identity theft when they notice that they are being billed for items they never purchased, or a credit account they never opened appears on their credit report.

Recent surveys estimate that nearly 10 million consumers are victimized by some form of identity theft each year. Many identity theft victims have reported that unauthorized persons have cleaned out their bank accounts, obtained credit in their name and, in some cases, have completely taken over their identities.

Victims of identity theft are not only victimized by the criminal who misappropriated their identity, but are further victimized by the system when their credit rating is ruined through no fault of their own as they try to undo the damage caused by unauthorized procurement of credit in their name.

Fortunately, the individual whose identity is stolen is often protected from financial loss by insurance or loss limits and reimbursement provisions. They nevertheless bear the tremendous emotional burden that identity theft causes, including loss to reputation, damage to their credit rating, and the time, nuisance, and out-of-pocket expenses of trying to clear their name.

Thus although the primary victim of identity theft is the individual whose personal information has been misused, the financial burden is often carried by the other "victims" of identity theft, such as the retail merchants, banks, utility companies and other credit grantors. In addition, taxpayers also indirectly bear some of this financial burden when social services are fraudulently obtained or when refunds are sent to individuals who file fraudulent tax returns.

As set forth in this Almanac, you must secure your computer, secure your e-mail, and take special precautions when shopping and conducting your financial transactions over the Internet. If you diligently follow all of this advice, you may think that you have successfully protected your personal information and, therefore, you are not a likely victim of identity theft.

Unfortunately, identity thieves are continually trying to find their way around all of the newest security devices, hacking their way through firewalls, and spreading viruses over the Internet. Never let your guard down when it comes to the potential for identity theft.

As discussed below, keep track of your credit card and bank accounts to make sure there is no suspicious activity or unauthorized charges. Review your credit report regularly to make sure there are no unauthorized accounts. Protecting yourself from identity theft requires that you diligently protect your personal information and act swiftly if you discover that your identity has been misused.

ADDITIONAL PREVENTION STRATEGIES

Identity thieves are constantly trying to intercept personal information that is shared on the Internet. They send e-mail messages to the victim, purportedly from the victim's Internet service provider, stating that the victim's "account information needs to be updated" or that the victim's "credit card is invalid or expired and the information needs to be reentered to keep the account active." If confronted with this message, the user is advised to contact their Internet service provider directly and not to divulge any personal information.

Although it may be impossible to completely prevent identity theft, you can minimize the risk by keeping careful track of your financial affairs and by cautiously guarding your personal information. When personal information is requested, find out how it is to be used and whether it will be shared with others. If possible, request that your information be kept confidential.

Do not give out personal information over the Internet unless you have initiated the contact, and you know who you are communicating with concerning the transaction. If you receive an unsolicited Internet contact, do not reveal any personal information.

Keep Track of Credit Accounts

It is also important to be familiar with your billing cycles and follow up with creditors if statements are missing or late. Make sure that your billing address has not been changed without your knowledge.

Review your credit cards statements as soon as you receive them. As discussed below, if you find any unauthorized purchases, report them to your creditor immediately and close the account and request a replacement credit card and new account number.

Use Secure Passwords

Make sure that you do not use passwords for online shopping and financial transactions that can be easily guessed, such as your date of birth or phone number, etc.

Protect Your Social Security Number

The Social Security Administration (SSA) is the only government agency authorized to issue social security numbers. An individual's social security number is a unique identifier of that person. This uniqueness, paired with the broad applicability of the social security number, has made it the identifier of choice for government agencies and private businesses.

In addition, the growth in computer technology over the past decades has prompted private businesses and government agencies to rely on social security numbers as a way to accumulate and identify information for their databases.

Therefore, the social security number is the most sought after piece of personal identification by individuals seeking to create false identities. Law enforcement officials and others consider the proliferation of false identities to be one of the fastest growing crimes today. According to the SSA, identity crime accounts for over 80 percent of social security number misuse allegations.

Stolen and counterfeit social security numbers have been used to gain employment, obtain benefits and services, establish credit, and to commit crimes. Using another's social security number, identity thieves have applied for and/or received government benefits such as supplemental security income, disability insurance, worker's compensation benefits, unemployment benefits, and public assistance.

This fraud has caused significant losses to government programs, credit card companies, and banks, and has caused consumers considerable time and out-of pocket expenses trying to clear their name and resolve the problems arising from the theft.

Therefore, you should be careful about sharing your number with anyone who asks for it, even when you are provided with a benefit or service. Knowing why the company wants your social security number will make it easier to decide whether or not to share this information. The Federal Trade Commission (FTC) advises consumers to ask the following questions if a company asks for a social security number:

1. Why do you need my social security number?

2. How will my social security number be used?

3. What law requires me to give you my social security number?

4. What will happen if I don't give you my social security number?

Identity thieves are often able to intercept one's social security number through unsecured websites on the Internet.

Secure Disposal of Your Old Computer

Computers often hold personal and financial information, including passwords, account numbers, license keys or registration numbers for software programs, addresses and phone numbers, medical and prescription information, tax returns, and other personal documents. This would provide a windfall of information for a potential identity thief. Thus if you plan to replace your old computer, it is important that you dispose of it in a secure manner.

Before getting rid of your old computer, you should use software to clean—i.e., erase—the hard drive. The computer's hard drive stores data, and maintains an index of files. When you save a file, especially a large one, it is scattered around the hard drive in bits and pieces. Files are also automatically created by browsers and operating systems. When you open a file, the hard drive checks the index, then gathers the bits and pieces and reconstructs them.

When you delete a file, the links between the index and the file disappear, signaling to your system that the file isn't needed any longer and that hard drive space can be overwritten. But the bits and pieces of the deleted file stay on your computer until they are overwritten, and can be retrieved with a data recovery program. To remove data from your hard drive permanently, it needs to be wiped clean.

Utility programs to clean the hard drive are available both online and in stores where computers are sold. These programs vary in their capabilities and effectiveness. It is best to choose a program that overwrites the hard drive numerous times as one time may not prevent all of the information from being recovered. Alternatively, you can remove the hard drive, and physically destroy it.

IF YOUR IDENTITY IS STOLEN

If, despite your efforts to protect your personal information, you are the unfortunate victim of identity theft, you must take immediate action to minimize the damage.

Report the Theft

Report the theft to your local police department. You must take immediate action because experienced identity thieves are aware that they have a limited time to run up your credit cards and misuse your identification, and they will act quickly.

Close Your Accounts

Close your bank and credit card accounts immediately and open new accounts. You should also contact the Department of Motor Vehicles and any other institution that issued identification cards, and follow their procedures for replacing lost or stolen identification.

Contact Credit Reporting Agencies

Place a preliminary fraud alert on your credit profiles with all three credit reporting agencies. It is also a good idea to review your credit report regularly to make sure you are aware of any changes as soon as possible after they occur. You must make sure your credit reports are accurate, up-to-date, and contain only authorized accounts. If you discover any unusual activity, incorrect addresses, or unauthorized accounts, report them immediately.

Under the Fair Credit Reporting Act (FCRA), you are entitled to receive a free copy of your credit report from each of the three nationwide consumer reporting agencies once every 12 months. The three consumer reporting agencies are Equifax, Experian and TransUnion. You should review all three reports as it is not unusual for there to be conflicting information on the reports.

You can order your free annual credit report by calling 1–877–322–8228, or online at: http://www.annualcreditreport.com. Alternatively, you can download and complete the Annual Credit Report Request form and mail it to:

> Annual Credit Report Request Service
> P.O. Box 105281
> Atlanta, Georgia 30348-5281

The FTC advises consumers who order their free annual credit reports online to be sure to correctly spell the website address, or link to it from the FTC's website to avoid being misdirected to other websites that offer supposedly free reports, but only with the purchase of other products. More importantly, you don't want to be redirected to a website that is trying to steal your personal information.

If you find errors in your report, or unauthorized accounts, you should contact the credit reporting agency directly. In order to order your credit reports, following is the contact information for the three major credit-reporting agencies:

EQUIFAX

> P.O. Box 740241
> Atlanta, GA 30374-0241
> Tel: 800-685-1111
> Website: http://www.equifax.com

EXPERIAN

> P.O. Box 2104
> Allen, TX 75013
> Tel: 888-EXPERIAN (888-397-3742)
> Website: http://www.experian.com

TRANSUNION

> P.O. Box 1000
> Chester, PA 19022
> Tel: 800-916-8800
> Website: http://www.transunion.com

The subject of identity theft is discussed more fully in this author's legal Almanac entitled *Identity Theft and How to Protect Yourself*, published by Oceana Publishing, a division of Oxford University Press.

APPENDIX 1:
THE ELECTRONIC COMMUNICATIONS PRIVACY ACT
[PUB. L. NO. 99-508, 10/21/86]

TITLE 18—CRIMES AND CRIMINAL PROCEDURE

PART 1—CRIMES

CHAPTER 119—WIRE AND ELECTRONIC COMMUNICATIONS
INTERCEPTION AND INTERECEPTION OF ORAL COMMUNICATIONS

SECTION 2510—DEFINITIONS

As used in this chapter—

(1) "Wire communication" means any aural transfer made in whole or in part through the use of facilities for the transmission of communications by the aid of wire, cable, or other like connection between the point of origin and the point of reception (including the use of such connection in a switching station) furnished or operated by any person engaged in providing or operating such facilities for the transmission of interstate or foreign communications for communications affecting interstate or foreign commerce and such term includes any electronic storage of such communication;

(2) "Oral communication" means any oral communication uttered by a person exhibiting an expectation that such communication is not subject to interception under circumstances justifying such expectation, but such term does not include any electronic communication;

(3) "State" means any State of the United States, the District of Columbia, the Commonwealth of Puerto Rico, and any territory or possession of the United States;

(4) "Intercept" means the aural or other acquisition of the contents of any wire, electronic, or oral communication through the use of any electronic, mechanical, or other device;

(5) "Electronic, mechanical, or other device" means any device or apparatus that can be used to intercept a wire, oral, or electronic communication other than—

(a) Any telephone or telegraph instrument, equipment or facility, or any component thereof, (I) furnished to the subscriber or user by a provider of wire or electronic communication service in the ordinary course of its business and being used by the subscriber or user in the ordinary course of its business or furnished by such subscriber or user for connection to the facilities of such service and used in the ordinary course of its business; or (ii) being used by a provider of wire or electronic communication service in the ordinary course of its business, or by an investigative or law enforcement officer in the ordinary course of his duties;

(b) A hearing aid or similar device being used to correct subnormal hearing to not better than normal;

(6) "Person" means any employee, or agent of the United States or any State or political subdivision thereof, and any individual, partnership, association, joint stock company, trust, or corporation;

(7) "Investigative or law enforcement officer" means any officer of the United States or of a State or political subdivision thereof, who is empowered by law to conduct investigations of or to make arrests for offenses enumerated in this chapter, and any attorney authorized by law to prosecute or participate in the prosecution of such offenses;

(8) "Contents," when used with respect to any wire, oral, or electronic communication, includes any information concerning the substance, purport, or meaning of that communication;

(9) "Judge of competent jurisdiction" means—

(a) A judge of a United States district court or a United States court of appeals; and

(b) A judge of any court of general criminal jurisdiction of a State who is authorized by a statute of that State to enter orders authorizing interceptions of wire, oral, or electronic communications;

(10) "Communication common carrier" shall have the same meaning which is given the term "common carrier" by section 153(h) of title 47 of the United States Code;

(11) "Aggrieved person" means a person who was a party to any intercepted wire, oral, or electronic communication or a person against whom the interception was directed;

(12) "Electronic communication" means any transfer of signs, signals, writing, images, sounds, data, or intelligence of any nature transmitted in whole or in part by a wire, radio, electromagnetic, photoelectronic or photooptical system that affects interstate or foreign commerce, but does not include—

(A) Any wire or oral communication;

(B) Any communication made through a tone-only paging device; or

(C) Any communication from a tracking device (as defined in section 3117 of this title);

(13) "User" means any person or entity who—

(A) Uses an electronic communication service; and

(B) Is duly authorized by the provider of such service

(14) "Electronic communications system" means any wire, radio, electromagnetic, photooptical or photoelectronic facilities for the transmission of electronic communications, and any computer facilities or related electronic equipment for the electronic storage of such communications;

(15) "Electronic communication service" means any service which provides to users thereof the ability to send or receive wire or electronic communications;

(16) "Readily accessible to the general public" means, with respect to a radio communication, that such communication is not—

(A) Scrambled or encrypted:

(B) Transmitted using modulation techniques whose essential parameters have been withheld from the public with the intention of preserving the privacy of such communication;

(C) Carried on a subcarrier or other signal subsidiary to a radio transmission;

(D) Transmitted over a communication system provided by a common carrier, unless the communication is a tone only paging system communication;

(E) Transmitted on frequencies allocated under part 25, subpart D, E, or F of part 74, or part 94 of the Rules of the Federal Communications Commission, unless, in the case of a communication transmitted on a frequency allocated under part 74 that is not exclusively allocated to broadcast auxiliary services, the communication is a two-way voice communication by radio; or

(F) An electronic communication;

(17) "Electronic storage" means—

(A) Any temporary, intermediate storage of a wire or electronic communication incidental to the electronic transmission thereof; and

(B) Any storage of such communication by an electronic communication service for purposes of backup protection of such communication; and

(18) "Aural transfer" means a transfer containing the human voice at any point between and including the point of origin and the point of reception.

SECTION 2510—INTERCEPTION AND DISCLOSURE OF WIRE, ORAL, OR ELECTRONIC COMMUNICATIONS PROHIBITED

(1) Except as otherwise specifically provided in this chapter any person who—

(a) intentionally intercepts, endeavors to intercept, or procures any other person to intercept or endeavor to intercept, any wire, oral, or electronic communication;

(b) intentionally uses, endeavors to use, or procures any other person to use or endeavor to use any electronic, mechanical, or other device to intercept any oral communication when—

(i) such device is affixed to, or otherwise transmits a signal through, a wire, cable, or other like connection used in wire communication; or

(ii) such device transmits communications by radio, or interferes with the transmission of such communication; or

(iii) such person knows, or has reason to know, that such device or any component thereof has been sent through the mail or transported in interstate or foreign commerce; or

(iv) such use or endeavor to use (A) takes place on the premises of any business or other commercial establishment the operations of which affect interstate or foreign commerce; or (B) obtains or is for the purpose of obtaining information relating to the operations of any business or other commercial establishment the operations of which affect interstate or foreign commerce; or

(v) such person acts in the District of Columbia, the Commonwealth of Puerto Rico, or any territory or possession of the United States;

(c) intentionally discloses, or endeavors to disclose, to any other person the contents of any wire, oral, or electronic communication, knowing or having reason to know that the information was obtained through the interception of a wire, oral, or electronic communication in violation of this subsection; or

(d) intentionally uses, or endeavors to use, the contents of any wire, oral, or electronic communication, knowing or having reason to know that the information was obtained through the interception of a wire, oral, or electronic communication in violation of this subsection; shall be punished as provided in subsection (4) or shall be subject to suit as provided in subsection (5).

(2)(a)(i) It shall not be unlawful under this chapter for an operator of a switchboard, or on officer, employee, or agent of a provider of wire or electronic communication service, whose facilities are used in the transmission of a wire communication, to intercept, disclose, or use that communication in the normal course of his employment while engaged in any activity which is a necessary incident to the rendition of his service or to the protection of the rights or property of the provider of that service, except that a provider of wire communication service to the public shall not utilize service observing or random monitoring except for mechanical or service quality control checks.

(ii) Notwithstanding any other law, providers of wire or electronic communication service, their officers, employees, and agents, landlords, custodians, or other persons, are authorized to provide information, facilities, or technical assistance to persons authorized by law to intercept wire, oral, or electronic communications or to conduct electronic surveillance, as defined in section 101 of the Foreign Intelligence Surveillance Act of 1978, if such provider, its officers, employees, or agents, landlord, custodian, or other specified person, has been provided with—

(A) a court order directing such assistance signed by the authorizing judge, or

(B) a certification in writing by a person specified in section 2518(7) of this title or the Attorney General of the United States that no warrant or court order is required by law, that all statutory requirements have been met, and that the specified assistance is required, setting forth the period of time during which the provision of the information, facilities, or technical assistance is authorized and specifying the information, facilities, or technical assistance required. No provider of wire or electronic communication service, officer, employee, or agent thereof, or landlord, custodian, or other specified person shall disclose the existence of any interception or surveillance or the device used to accomplish the interception or surveillance with respect to which the person has been furnished a court order or certification under this chapter, except as may otherwise be required by legal process and then only after prior notification to the Attorney General or to the principal prosecuting attorney of a State or any political subdivision of a State, as may be appropriate. Any such disclosure, shall render such person liable for the civil damages provided for in section 2520. No cause of action shall lie in any court against any provider of wire or electronic communication service, its officers, employees, or agents, landlord, custodian, or other specified person for providing information, facilities, or assistance in accordance with the terms of a court order or certification under this chapter.

(b) It shall not be unlawful under this chapter for an officer, employee, or agent of the Federal Communications Commission, in the normal course of his employment and in discharge of the monitoring responsibilities exercised by the Commission in the enforcement of chapter 5 of title 47 of the United States Code, to intercept a wire or electronic communication, or oral communication transmitted by radio, or to disclose or use the information thereby obtained.

(c) It shall not be unlawful under this chapter for a person acting under color of law to intercept a wire, oral, or electronic communication, where such person is a party to the communication or one of the parties to the communication has given prior consent to such interception.

(d) It shall not be unlawful under this chapter for a person not acting under color of law to intercept a wire, oral, or electronic communication where such person is a party to the communication or where one of the parties to the communication has given prior consent to such interception unless such communication is intercepted for the purpose of committing any criminal or tortious act in violation of the Constitution or laws of the United States or of any State.

(e) Notwithstanding any other provision of this title or section 705 or 706 of the Communications Act of 1934, it shall not be unlawful for an officer, employee, or agent of the United States in the normal course of his official duty to conduct electronic surveillance, as defined in section 101 of the Foreign Intelligence Surveillance Act of 1978, as authorized by that Act.

(f) Nothing contained in this chapter or chapter 121, or section 705 of the Communications Act of 1934, shall be deemed to affect the acquisition by the United States Government of foreign intelligence information from international or foreign communications, or foreign intelligence activities conducted in accordance with otherwise applicable Federal law involving a foreign electronic communications system, utilizing a means other than electronic surveillance as defined in section 101 of the Foreign Intelligence Surveillance Act of 1978, and procedures in this chapter and the Foreign Intelligence Surveillance Act of 1978 shall be the exclusive means by which electronic surveillance, as defined in section 101 of such Act, and the interception of domestic wire and oral communications may be conducted.

(g) It shall not be unlawful under this chapter or chapter 121 of this title for any person—

(i) to intercept or access an electronic communication made through an electronic communication system that is configured so that such electronic communication is readily accessible to the general public;

(ii) to intercept any radio communication which is transmitted—

(I) by any station for the use of the general public, or that relates to ships, aircraft, vehicles, or persons in distress;

(II) by any governmental, law enforcement, civil defense, private land mobile, or public safety communications system, including police and fire, readily accessible to the general public;

(III) by a station operating on an authorized frequency within the bands allocated to the amateur, citizens band, or general mobile radio services; or

(IV) by any marine or aeronautical communications system;

(iii) to engage in any conduct which—

(I) is prohibited by section 633 of the Communications Act of 1934; or

(II) is excepted from the application of section 705(a) of the Communications Act of 1934 by section 705(b) of that Act;

(iv) to intercept any wire or electronic communication the transmission of which is causing harmful interference to any lawfully operating station or consumer electronic equipment, to the extent necessary to identify the source of such interference; or

(v) for other users of the same frequency to intercept any radio communication made through a system that utilizes frequencies monitored by individuals engaged in the provision or the use of such system, if such communication is not scrambled or encrypted.

(h) It shall not be unlawful under this chapter—

(i) to use a pen register or a trap and trace device (as those terms are defined for the purposes of chapter 206 (relating to pen registers and trap and trace devices) of this title); or

(ii) for a provider of electronic communication service to record the fact that a wire or electronic communication was initiated or completed in order to protect such provider, another provider furnishing service toward the completion of the wire or electronic communication, or a user of that service, from fraudulent, unlawful or abusive use of such service.

(3)(a) Except as provided in paragraph (b) of this subsection, a person or entity providing an electronic communication service to the public shall not intentionally divulge the contents of any communication (other than one to such person or entity, or an agent thereof) while in transmission on that service to any person or entity other than an addressee or intended recipient of such communication or an agent of such addressee or intended recipient.

(b) A person or entity providing electronic communication service to the public may divulge the contents of any such communication—

(i) as otherwise authorized in section 2511(2)(a) or 2517 of this title;

(ii) with the lawful consent of the originator or any addressee or intended recipient of such communication;

(iii) to a person employed or authorized, or whose facilities are used, to forward such communication to its destination; or

(iv) which were inadvertently obtained by the service provider and which appear to pertain to the commission of a crime, if such divulgence is made to a law enforcement agency.

(4)(a) Except as provided in paragraph (b) of this subsection or in subsection (5), whoever violates subsection (1) of this section shall be fined under this title or imprisoned not more than five years, or both.

(b) If the offense is a first offense under paragraph (a) of this subsection and is not for a tortious or illegal purpose or for purposes of direct or indirect commercial advantage or private commercial gain, and the wire or electronic communication with respect to which the offense under paragraph (a) is a radio communication that is not scrambled or encrypted, then—

(i) if the communication is not the radio portion of a cellular telephone communication, a public land mobile radio service communication or a paging service communication, and the conduct is not that described in subsection (5), the offender shall be fined under this title or imprisoned not more than one year, or both; and

(ii) if the communication is the radio portion of a cellular telephone communication, a public land mobile radio service communication or a paging service communication, the offender shall be fined not more than $500.

(c) Conduct otherwise an offense under this subsection that consists of or relates to the interception of a satellite transmission that is not encrypted or scrambled and that is transmitted—

(i) to a broadcasting station for purposes of retransmission to the general public; or

(ii) as an audio subcarrier intended for redistribution to facilities open to the public, but not including data transmissions or telephone calls, is not an offense under this subsection unless the conduct is for the purposes of direct or indirect commercial advantage or private financial gain.

(5)(a)(i) If the communication is—

(A) a private satellite video communication that is not scrambled or encrypted and the conduct in violation of this chapter is the private viewing of that communication and is not for a tortious or illegal purpose or for purposes of direct or indirect commercial advantage or private commercial gain; or

(B) a radio communication that is transmitted on frequencies allocated under subpart D of part 74 of the rules of the Federal

Communications Commission that is not scrambled or encrypted and the conduct in violation of this chapter is not for a tortious or illegal purpose or for purposes of direct or indirect commercial advantage or private commercial gain, then the person who engages in such conduct shall be subject to suit by the Federal Government in a court of competent jurisdiction.

(ii) In an action under this subsection—

(A) if the violation of this chapter is a first offense for the person under paragraph (a) of subsection (4) and such person has not been found liable in a civil action under section 2520 of this title, the Federal Government shall be entitled to appropriate injunctive relief; and

(B) if the violation of this chapter is a second or subsequent offense under paragraph (a) of subsection (4) or such person has been found liable in any prior civil action under section 2520, the person shall be subject to a mandatory $500 civil fine.

(b) The court may use any means within its authority to enforce an injunction issued under paragraph (ii)(A), and shall impose a civil fine of not less than $500 for each violation of such an injunction.

***

SECTION 2520. RECOVERY OF CIVIL DAMAGES AUTHORIZED

(a) In general. Except as provided in section 2511(2)(a)(ii), any person whose wire, oral, or electronic communication is intercepted, disclosed, or intentionally used in violation of this chapter may in a civil action recover from the person or entity which engaged in that violation such relief as may be appropriate.

(b) Relief. In an action under this section, appropriate relief includes—

(1) such preliminary and other equitable or declaratory relief as may be appropriate;

(2) damages under subsection (c) and punitive damages in appropriate cases; and

(3) a reasonable attorney's fee and other litigation costs reasonably incurred.

(c) Computation of damages.

(1) In an action under this section, if the conduct in violation of this chapter is the private viewing of a private satellite video communication

that is not scrambled or encrypted or if the communication is a radio communication that is transmitted on frequencies allocated under subpart D of part 74 of the rules of the Federal Communications Commission that is not scrambled or encrypted and the conduct is not for a tortious or illegal purpose or for purposes of direct or indirect commercial advantage or private commercial gain, then the court shall assess damages as follows:

(A) If the person who engaged in that conduct has not previously been enjoined under section 2511(5) and has not been found liable in a prior civil action under this section, the court shall assess the greater of the sum of actual damages suffered by the plaintiff, or statutory damages of not less than $50 and not more than $500.

(B) If, on one prior occasion, the person who engaged in that conduct has been enjoined under section 2511(5) or has been found liable in a civil action under this section, the court shall assess the greater of the sum of actual damages suffered by the plaintiff, or statutory damages of not less than $100 and not more than $1000.

(2) In any other action under this section, the court may assess as damages whichever is the greater of

(A) the sum of the actual damages suffered by the plaintiff and any profits made by the violator as a result of the violation; or

(B) statutory damages of whichever is the greater of $100 a day for each day of violation or $10,000.

(d) Defense. A good faith reliance on—

(1) a court warrant or order, a grand jury subpoena, a legislative authorization, or a statutory authorization;

(2) a request of an investigative or law enforcement officer under section 2518(7) of this title; or

(3) a good faith determination that section 2511(3) of this title permitted the conduct complained of; is a complete defense against any civil or criminal action brought under this chapter or any other law.

(e) Limitation. A civil action under this section may not be commenced later than two years after the date upon which the claimant first has a reasonable opportunity to discover the violation.

APPENDIX 2:
THE PRIVACY PROTECTION ACT OF 1980
[42 U.S.C. § 2000aa]

THE PRIVACY PROTECTION ACT OF 1980 [42 U.S.C. § 2000aa 000aa]

SECTION 2000aa—SEARCHES AND SEIZURES BY GOVERNMENT OFFICERS AND EMPLOYEES IN CONNECTION WITH INVESTIGATION OR PROSECUTION OF CRIMINAL OFFENSES

(a) Work product materials

Notwithstanding any other law, it shall be unlawful for a government officer or employee, in connection with the investigation or prosecution of a criminal offense, to search for or seize any work product materials possessed by a person reasonably believed to have a purpose to disseminate to the public a newspaper, book, broadcast, or other similar form of public communication, in or affecting interstate or foreign commerce; but this provision shall not impair or affect the ability of any government officer or employee, pursuant to otherwise applicable law, to search for or seize such materials, if—

(1) there is probable cause to believe that the person possessing such materials has committed or is committing the criminal offense to which the materials relate: Provided, however, That a government officer or employee may not search for or seize such materials under the provisions of this paragraph if the offense to which the materials relate consists of the receipt, possession, communication, or withholding of such materials or the information contained therein (but such a search or seizure may be conducted under the provisions of this paragraph if the offense consists of the receipt, possession, or communication of information relating to the national defense, classified information, or restricted data under the provisions of

section 793, 794, 797, or 798 of title 18, or section 2274, 2275, or 2277 of this title, or section 783 of title 50, or if the offense involves the production, possession, receipt, mailing, sale, distribution, shipment, or transportation of child pornography, the sexual exploitation of children, or the sale or purchase of children under section 2251, 2251A, 2252, or 2252A of title 18); or

(2) there is reason to believe that the immediate seizure of such materials is necessary to prevent the death of, or serious bodily injury to, a human being.

Notwithstanding any other law, it shall be unlawful for a government officer or employee, in connection with the investigation or prosecution of a criminal offense, to search for or seize documentary materials, other than work product materials, possessed by a person in connection with a purpose to disseminate to the public a newspaper, book, broadcast, or other similar form of public communication, in or affecting interstate or foreign commerce; but this provision shall not impair or affect the ability of any government officer or employee, pursuant to otherwise applicable law, to search for or seize such materials, if—

(1) there is probable cause to believe that the person possessing such materials has committed or is committing the criminal offense to which the materials relate: Provided, however, That a government officer or employee may not search for or seize such materials under the provisions of this paragraph if the offense to which the materials relate consists of the receipt, possession, communication, or withholding of such materials or the information contained therein (but such a search or seizure may be conducted under the provisions of this paragraph if the offense consists of the receipt, possession, or communication of information relating to the national defense, classified information, or restricted data under the provisions of section 793, 794, 797, or 798 of title 18, or section 2274, 2275, or 2277 of this title, or section 783 of title 50, or if the offense involves the production, possession, receipt, mailing, sale, distribution, shipment, or transportation of child pornography, the sexual exploitation of children, or the sale or purchase of children under section 2251, 2251A, 2252, or 2252A of title 18);

(2) there is reason to believe that the immediate seizure of such materials is necessary to prevent the death of, or serious bodily injury to, a human being;

(3) there is reason to believe that the giving of notice pursuant to a subpoena duces tecum would result in the destruction, alteration, or concealment of such materials; or

(4) such materials have not been produced in response to a court order directing compliance with a subpoena duces tecum, and—

(A) all appellate remedies have been exhausted; or

(B) there is reason to believe that the delay in an investigation or trial occasioned by further proceedings relating to the subpoena would threaten the interests of justice.

(c) Objections to court ordered subpoenas; affidavits

In the event a search warrant is sought pursuant to paragraph (4)(B) of subsection (b) of this section, the person possessing the materials shall be afforded adequate opportunity to submit an affidavit setting forth the basis for any contention that the materials sought are not subject to seizure.

APPENDIX 3:
THE U.S.A. PATRIOT ACT—SELECTED PROVISIONS
[PUB. L. NO. 107-56, 10/26/01]

SECTION 1. SHORT TITLE AND TABLE OF CONTENTS.

(a) SHORT TITLE—This Act may be cited as the 'Uniting and Strengthening America by Providing Appropriate Tools Required to Intercept and Obstruct Terrorism (USA PATRIOT ACT) Act of 2001.'

ENHANCING DOMESTIC SECURITY AGAINST TERRORISM

SECTION 105. EXPANSION OF NATIONAL ELECTRONIC CRIME TASK FORCE INITIATIVE.

The Director of the United States Secret Service shall take appropriate actions to develop a national network of electronic crime task forces, based on the New York Electronic Crimes Task Force model, throughout the United States, for the purpose of preventing, detecting, and investigating various forms of electronic crimes, including potential terrorist attacks against critical infrastructure and financial payment systems.

TITLE II—ENHANCED SURVEILLANCE PROCEDURES

SECTION 201. AUTHORITY TO INTERCEPT WIRE, ORAL, AND ELECTRONIC COMMUNICATIONS RELATING TO TERRORISM.

Section 2516(1) of title 18, United States Code, is amended—

(1) by redesignating paragraph (p), as so redesignated by section 434(2) of the Antiterrorism and Effective Death Penalty Act of 1996 (Public Law 104-132; 110 Stat. 1274), as paragraph (r); and

(2) by inserting after paragraph (p), as so redesignated by section 201(3) of the Illegal Immigration Reform and Immigrant Responsibility Act of 1996 (division C of Public Law 104-208; 110 Stat. 3009–565), the following new paragraph:

'(q) any criminal violation of section 229 (relating to chemical weapons); or sections 2332, 2332a, 2332b, 2332d, 2339A, or 2339B of this title (relating to terrorism); or.'

SECTION 202. AUTHORITY TO INTERCEPT WIRE, ORAL, AND ELECTRONIC COMMUNICATIONS RELATING TO COMPUTER FRAUD AND ABUSE OFFENSES.

Section 2516(1)(c) of title 18, United States Code, is amended by striking 'and section 1341 (relating to mail fraud),' and inserting 'section 1341 (relating to mail fraud), a felony violation of section 1030 (relating to computer fraud and abuse),.'

SECTION 203. AUTHORITY TO SHARE CRIMINAL INVESTIGATIVE INFORMATION.

(b) AUTHORITY TO SHARE ELECTRONIC, WIRE, AND ORAL INTERCEPTION INFORMATION-

(1) LAW ENFORCEMENT- Section 2517 of title 18, United States Code, is amended by inserting at the end the following:

'(6) Any investigative or law enforcement officer, or attorney for the Government, who by any means authorized by this chapter, has obtained knowledge of the contents of any wire, oral, or electronic communication, or evidence derived therefrom, may disclose such contents to any other Federal law enforcement, intelligence, protective, immigration, national defense, or national security official to the extent that such contents include foreign intelligence or counterintelligence (as defined in section 3 of the National Security Act of 1947 (50 U.S.C. 401a)), or foreign intelligence information (as defined in subsection (19) of section 2510 of this title), to assist the official who is to receive that information in the performance of his official duties. Any Federal official who receives information pursuant to this provision may use that information only as necessary in the conduct of that person's official duties subject to any limitations on the unauthorized disclosure of such information.'

SECTION 204. CLARIFICATION OF INTELLIGENCE EXCEPTIONS FROM LIMITATIONS ON INTERCEPTION AND DISCLOSURE OF WIRE, ORAL, AND ELECTRONIC COMMUNICATIONS.

Section 2511(2)(f) of title 18, United States Code, is amended—

(1) by striking 'this chapter or chapter 121' and inserting 'this chapter or chapter 121 or 206 of this title'; and

(2) by striking 'wire and oral' and inserting 'wire, oral, and electronic.'

***

SECTION 209. SEIZURE OF VOICE-MAIL MESSAGES PURSUANT TO WARRANTS.

Title 18, United States Code, is amended—

(1) in section 2510—

(A) in paragraph (1), by striking beginning with 'and such' and all that follows through 'communication'; and

(B) in paragraph (14), by inserting 'wire or' after 'transmission of'; and

(2) in subsections (a) and (b) of section 2703—

(A) by striking 'CONTENTS OF ELECTRONIC' and inserting 'CONTENTS OF WIRE OR ELECTRONIC' each place it appears;

(B) by striking 'contents of an electronic' and inserting 'contents of a wire or electronic' each place it appears; and

(C) by striking 'any electronic' and inserting 'any wire or electronic' each place it appears.

SECTION 210. SCOPE OF SUBPOENAS FOR RECORDS OF ELECTRONIC COMMUNICATIONS.

Section 2703(c)(2) of title 18, United States Code, as redesignated by section 212, is amended—

(1) by striking 'entity the name, address, local and long distance telephone toll billing records, telephone number or other subscriber number or identity, and length of service of a subscriber' and inserting the following: 'entity the—

'(A) name;

'(B) address;

'(C) local and long distance telephone connection records, or records of session times and durations;

'(D) length of service (including start date) and types of service utilized;

'(E) telephone or instrument number or other subscriber number or identity, including any temporarily assigned network address; and

'(F) means and source of payment for such service (including any credit card or bank account number), of a subscriber'; and

(2) by striking 'and the types of services the subscriber or customer utilized,.'

SECTION 211. CLARIFICATION OF SCOPE.

Section 631 of the Communications Act of 1934 (47 U.S.C. 551) is amended—

(1) in subsection (c)(2)—

(A) in subparagraph (B), by striking 'or';

(B) in subparagraph (C), by striking the period at the end and inserting '; or'; and

(C) by inserting at the end the following:

'(D) to a government entity as authorized under chapters 119, 121, or 206 of title 18, United States Code, except that such disclosure shall not include records revealing cable subscriber selection of video programming from a cable operator.'; and

(2) in subsection (h), by striking 'A governmental entity' and inserting 'Except as provided in subsection (c)(2)(D), a governmental entity.'

SECTION 212. EMERGENCY DISCLOSURE OF ELECTRONIC COMMUNICATIONS TO PROTECT LIFE AND LIMB.

(a) DISCLOSURE OF CONTENTS-

(1) IN GENERAL- Section 2702 of title 18, United States Code, is amended—

(A) by striking the section heading and inserting the following:

'Sec. 2702. Voluntary disclosure of customer communications or records';

(B) in subsection (a)—

(i) in paragraph (2)(A), by striking 'and' at the end;

(ii) in paragraph (2)(B), by striking the period and inserting '; and'; and

(iii) by inserting after paragraph (2) the following:

'(3) a provider of remote computing service or electronic communication service to the public shall not knowingly divulge a record or other information pertaining to a subscriber to or customer of such service (not including the contents of communications covered by paragraph (1) or (2)) to any governmental entity.';

(C) in subsection (b), by striking 'EXCEPTIONS—A person or entity' and inserting 'EXCEPTIONS FOR DISCLOSURE OF COMMUNICATIONS- A provider described in subsection (a)';

(D) in subsection (b)(6)—

(i) in subparagraph (A)(ii), by striking 'or';

(ii) in subparagraph (B), by striking the period and inserting '; or'; and

(iii) by adding after subparagraph (B) the following:

'(C) if the provider reasonably believes that an emergency involving immediate danger of death or serious physical injury to any person requires disclosure of the information without delay.'; and

(E) by inserting after subsection (b) the following:

'(c) EXCEPTIONS FOR DISCLOSURE OF CUSTOMER RECORDS— A provider described in subsection (a) may divulge a record or other information pertaining to a subscriber to or customer of such service (not including the contents of communications covered by subsection (a)(1) or (a)(2))—

'(1) as otherwise authorized in section 2703;

'(2) with the lawful consent of the customer or subscriber;

'(3) as may be necessarily incident to the rendition of the service or to the protection of the rights or property of the provider of that service;

'(4) to a governmental entity if the provider reasonably believes that an emergency involving immediate danger of death or serious physical injury to any person justifies disclosure of the information; or

'(5) to any person other than a governmental entity..'

(2) TECHNICAL AND CONFORMING AMENDMENT—The table of sections for chapter 121 of title 18, United States Code, is amended by striking the item relating to section 2702 and inserting the following:

'2702. Voluntary disclosure of customer communications or records.'

(b) REQUIREMENTS FOR GOVERNMENT ACCESS—

(1) IN GENERAL—Section 2703 of title 18, United States Code, is amended—

(A) by striking the section heading and inserting the following:

'Sec. 2703. Required disclosure of customer communications or records';

(B) in subsection (c) by redesignating paragraph (2) as paragraph (3);

(C) in subsection (c)(1)—

(i) by striking '(A) Except as provided in subparagraph (B), a provider of electronic communication service or remote computing service may' and inserting 'A governmental entity may require a provider of electronic communication service or remote computing service to';

(ii) by striking 'covered by subsection (a) or (b) of this section) to any person other than a governmental entity.

'(B) A provider of electronic communication service or remote computing service shall disclose a record or other information pertaining to a subscriber to or customer of such service (not including the contents of communications covered by subsection (a) or (b) of this section) to a governmental entity' and inserting ')';

(iii) by redesignating subparagraph (C) as paragraph (2);

(iv) by redesignating clauses (i), (ii), (iii), and (iv) as subparagraphs (A), (B), (C), and (D), respectively;

(v) in subparagraph (D) (as redesignated) by striking the period and inserting '; or'; and

(vi) by inserting after subparagraph (D) (as redesignated) the following:

'(E) seeks information under paragraph (2).'; and

(D) in paragraph (2) (as redesignated) by striking 'subparagraph (B)' and insert 'paragraph (1).'

(2) TECHNICAL AND CONFORMING AMENDMENT—The table of sections for chapter 121 of title 18, United States Code, is amended by striking the item relating to section 2703 and inserting the following:

'2703. Required disclosure of customer communications or records..'

SECTION 213. AUTHORITY FOR DELAYING NOTICE OF THE EXECUTION OF A WARRANT.

Section 3103a of title 18, United States Code, is amended—

(1) by inserting '(a) IN GENERAL—'before 'In addition'; and

(2) by adding at the end the following:

'(b) DELAY—With respect to the issuance of any warrant or court order under this section, or any other rule of law, to search for and seize any property or material that constitutes evidence of a criminal offense in violation of the laws of the United States, any notice required, or that may be required, to be given may be delayed if—

'(1) the court finds reasonable cause to believe that providing immediate notification of the execution of the warrant may have an adverse result (as defined in section 2705);

'(2) the warrant prohibits the seizure of any tangible property, any wire or electronic communication (as defined in section 2510), or, except as expressly provided in chapter 121, any stored wire or electronic information, except where the court finds reasonable necessity for the seizure; and

'(3) the warrant provides for the giving of such notice within a reasonable period of its execution, which period may thereafter be extended by the court for good cause shown..'

***

SECTION 217. INTERCEPTION OF COMPUTER TRESPASSER COMMUNICATIONS.

Chapter 119 of title 18, United States Code, is amended—

(1) in section 2510—

(A) in paragraph (18), by striking 'and' at the end;

(B) in paragraph (19), by striking the period and inserting a semicolon; and

(C) by inserting after paragraph (19) the following:

'(20) 'protected computer' has the meaning set forth in section 1030; and

'(21) 'computer trespasser'—

'(A) means a person who accesses a protected computer without authorization and thus has no reasonable expectation of privacy in any communication transmitted to, through, or from the protected computer; and

'(B) does not include a person known by the owner or operator of the protected computer to have an existing contractual relationship with the owner or operator of the protected computer for access to all or part of the protected computer.'; and

(2) in section 2511(2), by inserting at the end the following:

'(i) It shall not be unlawful under this chapter for a person acting under color of law to intercept the wire or electronic communications of a computer trespasser transmitted to, through, or from the protected computer, if—

'(I) the owner or operator of the protected computer authorizes the interception of the computer trespasser's communications on the protected computer;

'(II) the person acting under color of law is lawfully engaged in an investigation;

'(III) the person acting under color of law has reasonable grounds to believe that the contents of the computer trespasser's communications will be relevant to the investigation; and

'(IV) such interception does not acquire communications other than those transmitted to or from the computer trespasser..'

***

SECTION 223. CIVIL LIABILITY FOR CERTAIN UNAUTHORIZED DISCLOSURES.

(a) Section 2520 of title 18, United States Code, is amended—

(1) in subsection (a), after 'entity,' by inserting ', other than the United States,';

(2) by adding at the end the following:

'(f) ADMINISTRATIVE DISCIPLINE—If a court or appropriate department or agency determines that the United States or any of its departments or agencies has violated any provision of this chapter, and the court or appropriate department or agency finds that the circumstances surrounding the violation raise serious questions about whether or not an officer or employee of the United States acted willfully or intentionally with respect to the violation, the department or agency shall, upon receipt of a true and correct copy of the decision and findings of the court or appropriate department or agency promptly initiate a proceeding to determine whether disciplinary action against the officer or employee is warranted. If the head of the department or agency involved determines that disciplinary action is not warranted, he or she shall notify the Inspector General with jurisdiction over the department or agency concerned and shall provide the Inspector General with the reasons for such determination.'; and

(3) by adding a new subsection (g), as follows:

'(g) IMPROPER DISCLOSURE IS VIOLATION—Any willful disclosure or use by an investigative or law enforcement officer or governmental entity of information beyond the extent permitted by section 2517 is a violation of this chapter for purposes of section 2520(a).'

APPENDIX 4:
SUMMARY OF FEDERAL PRIVACY LAWS

THE ADMINISTRATIVE PROCEDURES ACT [5 U.S.C. §§ 551, 554–558]

The Administrative Procedures Act establishes detailed procedures for Federal agencies to follow during administrative hearings. The Act's provisions prescribe, for example, the means by which agencies must notify individuals of their rights and liabilities, and how agencies may collect, present, and evaluate evidence and other data in such hearings.

THE CABLE COMMUNICATIONS POLICY ACT [47 U.S.C. § 551]

The Cable Communications Policy Act requires cable television operators to inform their subscribers annually about the nature of personal data collected, data disclosure practices, and subscriber rights to inspect and correct errors in such data. The Act prohibits a cable television company from using the cable system to collect personal information about its subscribers without their prior consent, and generally bars the cable operator from disclosing such data. The Act authorizes damage awards of at least $1,000, and awards of punitive damages, costs, and attorneys' fees against cable television companies that violate the Act's subscriber privacy provisions.

THE CENSUS CONFIDENTIAL STATUTE [13 U.S.C. § 9]

The Census Confidentiality Statute prohibits any use of census data for other than the original statistical purpose. The statute also prohibits any disclosure of census data that would allow an individual to be identified, except to sworn officers and employees of the Census Bureau.

THE CHILDREN'S ONLINE PRIVACY PROTECTION ACT OF 1998 [15 U.S.C. §§ 6501 et seq.; 16 C.F.R. § 312]

The Children's Online Privacy Protection Act of 1998 requires a website directed at children under 13 years of age to obtain "verifiable parental consent" before collecting personal information online from children. The COPPA regulation defines the term "collects" to encompass providing a child with the ability to have an e-mail account or the ability to post to a chat room, bulletin board, or other online forum. The COPPA also requires a covered Web site to disclose in a notice its online information collection and use practices with respect to children, and provide parents with the opportunity to review the personal information collected online from their children.

THE COMMUNICATIONS ASSISTANCE FOR LAW ENFORCEMENT STATUTE [47 U.S.C. § 1001]

The Communications Assistance for Law Enforcement Statute reserves law enforcement's ability to engage in lawful electronic surveillance in the face of new technological developments. The statute increases the protections against governmental intrusions into the privacy of electronic communications and requires that the government obtain a court order before obtaining tracking information or location information about subscribers from mobile service providers, and explicitly states that it does not limit the rights of subscribers to use encryption.

THE COMPUTER SECURITY ACT [40 U.S.C. § 1441]

The Computer Security Act protects data maintained in government computers and requires each Federal agency to provide mandatory training in computer security awareness.

THE CONSUMER CREDIT REFORM ACT OF 1996 [Pub. L. NO. 104-208, 9/30/96]

The Consumer Credit Reporting Reform Act of 1996 (Reform Act) overhauled the Fair Credit Reporting Act (see below). The Reform Act requires more frequent and fuller notification to consumers, disclosure of all information, rather than only the substance of the information, in the consumer's file, and stricter reinvestigation when a consumer disputes the accuracy of information in his or her file. Imposes new restrictions on resellers of consumer credit reports and strengthens private enforcement rights for violations of the Fair Credit Reporting Act.

THE CRIMINAL JUSTICE INFORMAITON SYSTEMS STATUTE
[42 U.S.C. § 3789G]

The Criminal Justice Information Systems Statute requires Federally-funded State and local criminal justice information systems to include information on the disposition of any arrest and permits individuals to see, copy, and correct information about themselves in the system.

THE CUSTOMER PROPRIETARY NETWORK INFORMATION STATUTE
[47 U.S.C. § 222]

The Customer Proprietary Network Information Statute restricts private sector access and use of customer data, and the disclosure of individualized customer data obtained for purposes of providing telecommunications service absent customer approval. The statute imposes restrictions on the use of such data in aggregate form.

THE DRIVER'S PRIVACY PROTECTION ACT [18 U.S.C. § 2721]

The Driver's Privacy Protection Act prohibits State Departments of Motor Vehicles (DMVs) from releasing "personal information" from drivers' licenses and motor vehicle registration records. Permits the release of the information to recipients who are using it for one or more specific statutory purposes, or where the subject of the record was furnished with an opportunity to limit the release of the information and did not do so. The Act penalizes the procurement of information from motor vehicle records for an unlawful purpose, or the making of a false representation to obtain such information from a DMV. The Act imposes a record keeping requirement on the resellers of such information. The Act does not interfere with the ability of states to enact laws furnishing greater privacy protection to their drivers and vehicle owners.

THE DRUG AND ALCOHOLISM ABUSE CONFIDENTIALITY STATUTE
[21 U.S.C. § 290dd-3]

The Drug and Alcoholism Abuse Confidentiality Statute prohibit disclosure of information collected for federally-funded research and treatment of drug abuse and alcoholism. The statute also prohibits use of this information for any purpose outside of the research or treatment program, except in cases of medical emergency or where a court order has been issued. Such information is specifically protected from use against the subject of any criminal proceeding. Violators of the statute are subject to a fine.

THE ELECTRONIC COMMUNICATIONS PRIVACY ACT
[18 U.S.C. § 2701 et seq.]

The Electronic Communications Privacy Act prohibits persons from tampering with computers or accessing certain computerized records without authorization. The Act also prohibits providers of electronic communications services from disclosing the contents of stored communications. The Act usually requires that the customer be notified and given an opportunity to contest in court a government entity's request for access to electronic mail or other stored communications in the control of a provider of electronic communications services or remote computing services.

THE ELECTRONIC FUNDS TRANSFER ACT [15 U.S.C. §§ 1693; 1693m]

The Electronic Funds Transfer Act requires banks to make extensive disclosures to customers about specific electronic funds transfer (EFT) transactions, both at the time the transactions are made and in the form of periodic statements. The Act requires banks to notify customers, at the time they contract for EFT services, of their rights, liabilities, charges, procedures, etc., connected with the services, and of whom to contact if an unauthorized transfer is suspected. In the case of preauthorized periodic transfers—such as automatic bill paying—the bank must provide either positive or negative notice as to whether payments are being made on schedule. The Act mandates detailed procedures for the resolution of any inaccuracies in customer accounts, and imposes liability on the bank for errors in the transmission or documentation of transfers. An individual who prevails in a civil action for a violation of the Act may recover actual damages sustained, a penalty of $100 to $1,000, attorney's fees and court costs, and in limited situations, treble damages. Criminal penalties may be imposed for deliberate violations of the Act. Numerous federal agencies also have administrative responsibility for enforcing the provisions of this Act.

THE EMPLOYEE POLYLGRAPH PROTECTION AC [29 U.S.C. § 2001 et seq.]

The Employee Polygraph Protection Act prohibits employers from requiring a polygraph test as a condition of employment or using the results of such tests as the sole basis for disciplining employees or taking other adverse employment actions. The Act bars employers from publicly disclosing the results of polygraph tests unless disclosure is made to the government pursuant to a court order or for the purpose of providing the government with information on criminal conduct. Employers that violate the Act may be subject to a fine of up to $10,000, injunctive relief such as employee reinstatements, and awards of damages, costs and attorneys' fees.

THE EMPLOYEE RETIREMENT INCOME SECURITY ACT [29 U.S.C. § 1025]

The Employee Retirement Income Security Act requires employers to provide employees with access to information about their accrued retirement benefits.

THE EQUAL CREDIT OPPORTUNITY ACT [15 U.S.C. § 1691 et seq.]

The Equal Credit Opportunity Act restricts inquiries into a credit applicant's sex, race, color, religion, or marital status. The Act prohibits the retention and preservation of certain information by creditors and requires the preservation of certain specified records relating to credit transactions. The Act regulates the manner in which information collected by creditors may be used in making decisions regarding the extension of credit. The Act requires that, when credit is denied or revoked, the applicant must be either notified of the reasons for the decision or informed of his right to learn the reasons. In suits brought for violations of the Equal Credit Opportunity Act, successful plaintiffs may recover actual damages, punitive damages, attorneys' fees and court costs. Individual or class action suits may be maintained for administrative, injunctive or declaratory relief. Numerous Federal agencies also have enforcement responsibility for the provisions of this Act.

THE EQUAL EMPLOYMENT OPPORTUNITY ACT [42 U.S.C. § 2000E et seq.]

The Equal Employment Opportunity Act restricts collection and use of information that would result in employment discrimination on the basis of race, sex, religion, national origin and a variety of other characteristics.

THE FAIR CREDIT BILLING ACTG [15 U.S.C. § 1666]

The Fair Credit Billing Act requires creditors, at the request of individual consumers, to investigate alleged billing errors and to provide documentary evidence of the individual's indebtedness. The Act prohibits creditors from taking action against individuals with respect to disputed debts while disputes are under investigation. Any creditor who fails to disclose required information is subject to a civil suit, with a minimum penalty of $100 and a maximum penalty of $1,000 on any individual credit transaction. The Act also imposes criminal liability on any person who knowingly and willfully gives false or inaccurate information, fails to disclose required information, or otherwise violates any requirement imposed by the Act. Any such person is subject to a fine of $5,000 and/or imprisonment for not more than one year.

THE FAIR CREDIT REPORTING ACT [15 U.S.C. § 1681 et seq.]

The Fair Credit Reporting Act regulates the collection and use of personal data by credit reporting agencies. The Act requires that when a data broker is hired to prepare an "investigative consumer report"—i.e., an investigation into the consumer's "character, general reputation, personal characteristics or mode of living" by means of interviews with friends, neighbors and associates—the request for information must be disclosed to the subject of the report, who is then entitled to learn the nature and scope of the inquiry requested. The Act requires that, if a consumer report is used in any decision to deny credit, insurance or employment, the report user must tell the consumer the name and address of the reporting agency. The Act prohibits disclosure of consumer reports maintained by consumer reporting agencies without consent unless such disclosure is made for a legitimate business purpose or pursuant to a court order. The Act requires reporting agencies to use procedures that will avoid reporting specified categories of obsolete information and to verify information in investigative consumer reports that are used more than once. The Act requires brokers to maintain security procedures, including procedures to verify the identity and stated purposes of recipients of consumer reports. Individuals may sue credit reporting agencies or parties who obtain consumer reports for violations of the Act. Individuals may recover for actual damages suffered, as well as attorneys' fees and court costs. Punitive damages or criminal penalties may also be imposed for willful violations of the Act. The Federal Trade Commission and other Federal agencies responsible for enforcing the provisions of this Act are also empowered to declare actions to be in violation of the applicable statute, issue cease and desist orders, and impose statutory penalties for noncompliance with agency orders.

THE FAIR DEBT COLLECTION PRACTICES ACT [15 U.S.C. § 1692 et seq.]

The Fair Debt Collection Practices Act limits the communications that debt collection agencies may make about the debtors whose accounts they are attempting to collect. The Act imposes liability on debt collectors for any actual damages sustained, as well as additional damages not to exceed $1,000, court costs and attorneys' fees. Numerous Federal agencies also have administrative responsibility for enforcing the provisions of this Act.

THE FAIR HOUSING ACT [42 U.S.C. §§ 3604; 3605]

The Fair Housing Statute restricts the collection and use of information that would result in housing discrimination on the basis of race, sex, religion, national origin and a variety of other factors.

THE FAMILY EDUCATIONAL RIGHTS AND PRIVACY ACT [20 U.S.C. 1232g]

The Family Educational Rights and Privacy Act permits a student or the parent of a minor student to inspect and challenge the accuracy and completeness of educational records which concern the student. The Act prohibits schools receiving public funds from using or disclosing the contents of a student's records without the consent of the student or of the parent of the minor student. The Act prohibits government access to personal data in educational records without a court order or lawfully issued subpoena, unless the government is seeking access to the records for a specified education-related purpose. The Act vests administrative enforcement in the Department of Education, and provides for termination of Federal funds if an institution violates the Act and compliance cannot be secured voluntarily.

THE FREEDOM OF INFORMATION ACT (FOIA) [5 U.S.C. § 552]

Freedom of Information Act provides individuals with access to many types of records that are exempt from access under the Privacy Act, including many categories of personal information. Unlike those of the Privacy Act, FOIA procedures are available to non-resident foreign nationals.

THE GRAMM-LEACH-BLILEY ACT [15 U.S.C. §§ 6801 et seq.]

The Gramm-Leach-Bliley Act regulates the privacy of personally identifiable, nonpublic financial information disclosed to non-affiliated third parties by financial institutions. Requirements also attach to non-affiliated third parties to whom they transfer this information. The Act requires written or electronic notice of the categories of nonpublic personal information collected, categories of people to whom the information will be disclosed, consumer opt-out rights, and the company's confidentiality and security policies. The Act creates consumer right to opt out of disclosures to nonaffiliated parties before the disclosure occurs, subject to a long list of exceptions. The Act requires administrative, technical and physical safeguards to maintain the security, confidentiality, and integrity of the information. The Act generally prohibits disclosure of account numbers and access codes for credit, deposit or transaction accounts to a nonaffiliated party for marketing purposes.

THE HEALTH INSURANCE PORTABILITY AND ACCOUNTABILITY ACT [PUB. L. NO. 104-191 §§ 262–264; C.F.R. §§ 160–164]

The Health Insurance Portability and Accountability Act is a Department of Health and Human Services regulation, which goes into effect in 2003, and applies to individually identifiable health information that has been maintained or transmitted by a covered entity. The Act applies directly to three types of entities: health plans, health care providers, and health care clearinghouses. The Act will also require these covered entities to apply many of its provisions to their business associates, including contractors, third-party administrators, researchers, life insurance issuers and employers. The Act requires health plans and health care providers to provide a written notice of how protected health information about an individual will be used, as well as an accounting of the circumstances surrounding certain disclosures of the information. The Act prohibits covered entities from disclosing covered information in a manner inconsistent with the notice. The Act requires covered entities to obtain a patient's opt-in via "consent" form for both use and disclosure of protected information for treatment, payment or health care operations. The Act also requires covered entities to obtain a patient's more detailed opt in via an "authorization" form for both use and disclosure of protected information for purposes other than treatment, payment or health care operations. The Act permits several forms of marketing and fundraising uses of protected information subject to receipt of written consent and subsequent provision of opportunity to opt out. The Act requires patient authorization for transfers of protected information for routine marketing by third parties. The Act provides right to access, copy and amend the information in designated record sets, including in a business associate's records if not a duplicate of the information held by the provider or plan.

THE HEALTH RESEARCH DATA STATUTE [42 U.S.C. § 242m]

The Health Research Data Statute prohibits disclosure of data collected by the National Centers for Health Services Research and for Health Statistics that would identify an individual in any way.

THE MAIL PRIVACY STATUTE [39 U.S.C. § 3623]

The Mail Privacy Statute prohibits opening of mail without a search warrant or the addressee's consent.

THE PAPERWORK REDUCTION ACT OF 1980 [44 U.S.C. § 3501 et seq.]

The Paperwork Reduction Act prohibits an agency from collecting information from the public if another agency has already collected the same information, or if the Office of Management and Budget does not believe the agency either needs or can make use of the information. The Act requires each Federal data collection form to explain why the information is being collected, how it is to be used, and whether the individual's response is mandatory, required to obtain a benefit, or voluntary.

THE PRIVACY ACT [5 U.S.C. § 552a]

The Privacy Act mandates that personal data be collected as much as possible directly from the record subject. Generally prohibits collection of information about an individual's exercise of First Amendment rights (e.g., freedom of expression, assembly, and religion). The Act requires that when an agency requests information about an individual, it notify the individual of the agency's authorization and purpose for collecting information, the extra-agency disclosures ("routine uses") that may be made of the data collected, and the consequences to the individual for failing to provide the information. The Act requires agencies, on request, to provide individuals with access to records pertaining to them and an opportunity to correct or challenge the contents of the records.

The Privacy Act restricts Federal agencies from disclosing personal data except for publicly announced purposes, and requires agencies to (1) keep an accounting of extra-agency disclosures; to (2) instruct record management personnel in the requirements of the Act and the rules for its implementation; and (3) "establish appropriate administrative, technical, and physical safeguards to insure the security and confidentiality of records." The Act places accountability for the handling of personal records on the record-keeping agency and its employees. The Act requires agencies to publish a detailed annual notice that describe each record system, the kind of information maintained, its sources, the policies governing management of the system, and the procedures for individuals to obtain access to records about themselves. The Act allows an individual harmed by a violation to sue the agency for an injunction, damages, and court costs. It also provides criminal penalties—fines of up to $5,000—against employees who disclose records in violation of the Act.

THE PRIVACY PROTECTION ACT [42 U.S.C. § 2000aa]

The Privacy Protection Act prohibits government agents from conducting unannounced searches of press offices and files if no one in the press office is suspected of a crime. The Act requires instead that the government request voluntary cooperation or subpoena the material sought, giving the holder of the material a chance to contest the action in court. The Act directs the U.S. Attorney General to issue guidelines for seeking evidence from other non-suspect third parties, with special consideration to such traditionally confidential relationships as doctor-patient and priest-penitent.

THE RIGHT TO FINANCIAL PRIVACY ACT [12 U.S.C. § 3401 et seq.]

The Right to Financial Privacy Act requires Federal agencies seeking access to private financial records either: (1) to notify the subject of the purpose for which the records are sought and provide the subject with an opportunity to challenge the disclosure in court; or (2) to obtain a court order for direct access to the records if notice would allow the record subject to flee or destroy the evidence. The Act prohibits a Federal agency that has obtained access to an individual's financial records from disclosing the records to another agency without: (1) notifying the individual; and (2) obtaining certification from the receiving agency that the records are relevant to a legitimate law enforcement inquiry of the receiving agency. Where a government agency or a financial institution discloses records or information in violation of the Right to Financial Privacy Act, the agency or institution is liable to the customer for any actual damages sustained, a $100 penalty, punitive damages for willful or intentional violations, court costs, and attorney's fees.

THE TAX REFORM ACT [26 U.S.C. §§ 6103; 7609]

The Tax Reform Act requires notice and opportunity- to-challenge procedures (similar to those of the Right to Financial Privacy Act) before the Internal Revenue Service may obtain access to certain institutional records about an individual in the hands of certain private record keepers. The Act strictly limits disclosure of tax returns and return information, and in some cases requires a court order for disclosures to law enforcement agencies for purposes unrelated to tax administration.

THE TELEPHONE CONSUMER PROTECTION ACT [47 U.S.C. § 227]

The Telephone Consumer Protection Act (47 U.S.C. § 227) The Telephone Consumer Protection Act requires entities wh use the telephone to solicit individuals, to provide such individuals with the ability to prevent future telephone solicitations. The Act requires those who engage in telephone solicitations to maintain and honor lists of individuals who request not to receive such solicitations for ten years. The Act prohibits unsolicited commercial telephone calls using an artificial or pre-recorded voice without consumer consent, and prohibits the sending of unsolicited advertisements to facsimile machines.

THE VIDEO PRIVACY PROTECTION ACT [18 U.S.C. § 2710]

The Video Privacy Protection Act affords users and purchasers of commercial videotapes rights similar to those of patrons of libraries. The Act prohibits videotape sale or rental companies from disclosing customer names and addresses, and the subject matter of their purchases or rentals for direct marketing use, unless the customers have been notified of their right to prohibit such disclosures. The Act restricts videotape companies from disclosing personal data about customers without customers' consent or court approval. The Act requires that subscribers be notified and provided with an opportunity to contest a data request prior to a judicial determination. Video companies that violate the Video Privacy Protection Act may be liable for damage awards of at least $2500, punitive damages, costs and attorneys' fees.

WIRETAP STATUTESA [18 U.S.C. § 2510 et seq.; 47 U.S.C. § 605]

Wiretap Statutes prohibit the use of eavesdropping technology and the interception of electronic mail, radio communications, data transmission and telephone calls without consent. The Federal Communications Commission also has a rule and tariff prescription prohibiting the recording of telephone conversations without notice or consent.

APPENDIX 5:
SUMMARY OF STATE PRIVACY LAWS

BANK RECORDS STATUTES

Bank records statutes prohibit financial institutions from disclosing financial records of a customer to a third party without legal process or customer consent.

CABLE TELEVISION STATUTES

Cable television statutes permit subscribers to correct information or have their names deleted from data files maintained by cable operators. These statutes prohibit disclosure of personal information collected by a cable operator unless the subscriber has had notice and has not objected to the disclosure.

COMMON LAW REMEDIES

Common law remedies provide redress for invasion of privacy—i.e., intrusions into places of affairs as to which an individual has a reasonable expectation of privacy—public disclosure of privacy facts, defamation—i.e., disclosures of inaccurate personal information—and breach of duty of confidentiality. These remedies generally provide for money damages and, in some cases, nominal, special or punitive damages, and injunctive relief.

COMPUTER CRIME STATUTES

Computer crime statutes prohibit individuals from tampering with computers or accessing certain computerized records without authorization. Persons engaged in such conduct are subject to criminal penalties, civil damages or both.

CREDIT REPORTING STATUTES

Credit reporting statutes prohibit collection by creditors of information on race, religion, or sex. These statutes also restrict disclosure by credit reporting agencies of credit information to third parties.

CRIMINAL JUSTICE INFORMATION STATUTES

Criminal justice information statutes require law enforcement agencies to permit individuals to see, copy, and correct information about themselves maintained in the criminal justice information systems. These statutes require that criminal justice information be reported promptly, completely, and in standard format. These statues also have quality control requirements for computerized information systems and special requirements that arrest records indicate the disposition of the case. In addition, most of the State criminal justice information statutes require strict security measures to protect this information.

EMPLOYMENT RECORDS STATUTES

Employment records statutes prohibit employers from collecting information about a job applicant's race, sex, color, religion, national origin, and other attributes. These statutes allow individuals access to personnel records held by their employers.

FAIR INFORMATION PRACTICES STATUTES

Fair information practices statutes limit the type of information that State governments can collect and maintain about individuals. These statutes allow individuals to inspect and challenge information about them held by the State. Restrict the ability of State governments to disclose personal data to third parties.

GENETIC INFORMATION STATUTES

Genetic information statutes limit use of genetic information for therapeutic or diagnostic purposes. These statutes prohibit use of information as a condition to determine eligibility for health, disability, life or other forms of insurance.

INSURANCE RECORDS STATUTES

Insurance records statutes require insurers to provide general information about their personal data practices to applicants and policyholders, with further information available upon request. These statutes require them to notify applicants about the collection and disclosure of personal data, and to specify when information is requested solely for marketing or research purposes. These statutes restrict the use of "pretext interviews," in which the identity or purpose of the interviewer is misrepresented, and require specific consent forms to be used for the collection of information that requires authorization from an individual. These statutes permit individuals who are denied insurance to learn the specific reasons for such denial and to obtain access to the information used in refusing coverage. Applicants or policyholders also may obtain access to non-privileged personal information about them, and may propose that such information be corrected, amended or deleted. Except where such disclosure is permitted by law, these statutes prohibit insurers from disclosing (without the individual's consent) information they collect on individuals.

MEDIA SHIELD STATUTES

Media shield statutes permit journalists to refuse to identify the sources of information received in the course of professional employment.

MEDICAL RECORDS STATUTES

Medical records statutes allow individuals to have access to their medical records. These statutes limit the use and disclosure of medical or mental health records.

POLYGRAPH TEST STATUTES

Polygraph test statutes restrict the use of mandatory polygraph tests as a condition for employment.

PRIVILEGE STATUTES

Privilege statutes limit the introduction into legal proceedings of personal information maintained by professionals such as doctors, psychotherapists, attorneys, clergy and accountants, concerning individuals with whom they have a professional relationship.

SCHOOL RECORDS STATUTES

School records statutes permit students and their parents to inspect and challenge the accuracy and completeness of school records. Limit the ability of schools to disclose information from school records to third parties.

STORED WIRE COMMUNICATIONS STATUTES

Stored wire communications statutes require notice to subscribers before the government can access stored wire communications.

TAX RETURN STATUTES

Tax Return Statutes prohibit disclosure by the government of State tax returns and return information.

TELEPHONE/FACSIMILES SOLICITATION STATUTES

Telephone/facsimile solicitation statutes restricts home telephone solicitations from using recorded messages; limits unsolicited fax advertisements.

THE UNIFORM COMMERCIAL CODE

The Uniform Commercial Code encourages financial institutions to disclose to their customers in a timely fashion the record of all transactions by holding the financial institution responsible for any errors until after the customer is informed of the bank's version of what has occurred.

VIDEO PRIVACY STATUTES

Video privacy statutes restrict videotape sales or rental companies from disclosing personal data about customers without their consent.

WIRETAP STATUTES

Wiretap statutes restrict electronic eavesdropping and interception of communications by wire or radio. Some states also have tariff prescriptions requiring common carriers operating within their jurisdictions to terminate subscribers who record telephone conversations without notice or consent.

SOURCE: The Better Business Bureau (BBB).

APPENDIX 6:
INTERNET PRIVACY RESOURCE
DIRECTORY

ORGANIZATION	WEBSITE	FUNCTION	SERVICES
AMERICA LINKS UP	www.americalinksup.org	Child online protection organization	Public awareness and education campaign sponsored by a broad-based coalition of non-profits organizations, education groups, and corporations concerned with providing children with a safe and rewarding online experience
AMERICAN CIVIL LIBERTIES UNION (ACLU)	www.acllu.org	Advocacy organization	Advocates individual rights by litigating, legislating, and educating the public on a broad array of issues affecting individual freedom in the United States; founding member of the Global Internet Liberty Campaign, an international coalition of organizations dedicated to protecting freedom of speech and the right to privacy in cyberspace
ASSOCIATION FOR INTERACTIVE MEDIA (AIM)	www.interactivehq.org	Trade organization	Non-profit trade association for business users of the Internet which includes companies that are committed to maximizing the value of the Internet to businesses and consumers

ORGANIZATION	WEBSITE	FUNCTION	SERVICES
BETTER BUSINESS BUREAU (BBB)	www.bbb.org	Business watch organization	Operates an authenticated and verified "seal" program that helps consumers find reliable companies that pledge to meet tough advertising and dispute settlement standards, including responsible advertising to children
CALL FOR ACTION	www.callforaction.org	Consumer information hotline	International network of free consumer hotlines to assist consumer in resolving and mediating fraud and privacy disputes
CENTER FOR DEMOCRACY AND TECHNOLOGY (CDT)	www.cdt.org	Advocacy organization	Works to promote democratic values and constitutional liberties in the digital age; seeks practical solutions to enhance free expression and privacy in global communications technologies; dedicated to building consensus among all parties interested in the future of the Internet and other new communications media; offers its "Operation Opt-Out," which allows users to easily generate form letters to be taken out of mailing lists
CENTER FOR MEDIA EDUCATION	www.cme.org	Child online protection organization	Non-profit organization dedicated to improving the quality of electronic media, especially on the behalf of children and families; involved in investigating the children's online marketplace

ORGANIZATION	WEBSITE	FUNCTION	SERVICES
CHILDREN'S ADVERTISING REVIEW UNIT (CARU)	www.bbb.org/advertising/childrensmonitor.asp	Child online protection organization	First organization to develop self-regulatory guidelines for businesses advertising to children online; provides voluntary standards for the protection of children under the age of 12 including information on the disclosure of what information is being collected and its intended uses and the opportunity for the consumer to withhold consent for information collection for marketing purposes
CONSUMER ACTION	www.consumer-action.org	Advocacy organization	Membership-based organization concerned with advancing consumer rights, referring consumers to complaint-handling agencies through its free hotline, publishing multilingual educational materials, and advocating for consumers in the media and before lawmakers
CONSUMER PRIVACY GUIDE	www.consumerprivacyguide.org	Information service	Site offers extensive tips, a glossary of terms, and video tutorials with step-by-step instructions on how to take advantage of privacy settings for the programs you use online
CPA WEBTRUST	www.cpawebtrust.org	Online oversight organization	CPA firms verify security systems of participating websites every 90 days and award icons of approval
CYBERANGELS	www.cyberangels.org	Child online protection organization	Finds and reports illegal material online; educates families about online safety; works with schools and libraries; and shares basic internet tips and help resources

ORGANIZATION	WEBSITE	FUNCTION	SERVICES
DIRECT MARKETING ASSOCIATION (DMA)	www.the-dma.org	Opting out service	Offers information on online marketing protections and advice on getting rid of unsolicited commercial e-mail; tells consumer how to delete their name from e-mail marketing lists and includes downloadable forms; peer review process acts on consumer complaints about DMA members and nonmembers
ELECTRONIC FRONTIER FOUNDATION (EFF)	www.eff.org	Advocacy organization	Nonprofit organization working to guarantee that all civil liberties are protected on the Internet and in all digital communication arenas; provides a free telephone hotline for questions regarding legal rights, and will answer your technical and legal questions via telephone, snail mail, and e-mail
ELECTRONIC PRIVACY INFORMATION CENTER (EPIC)	www.epic.org	Advocacy organization	Nonprofit organization established to focus public attention on emerging civil liberties issues and to protect privacy and constitutional values
EQUIFAX	www.equifax.com	Credit reporting organization	One of the three major national credit reporting agencies where the consumer can order a copy of their credit report online; read fraud FAQs; and find out how to report credit card misuse or remove their name from pre-approved credit card offer mailing lists

ORGANIZATION	WEBSITE	FUNCTION	SERVICES
EXPERIAN	www.experian.com	Credit reporting organization	One of the three major national credit reporting agencies where the consumer can order a copy of their credit report online; read fraud FAQs; and find out how to report credit card misuse or remove their name from pre-approved credit card offer mailing lists
FEDERAL TRADE COMMISSION (FTC)	www.ftc.gov	Government organization	Provides a wealth of information on current privacy legislation and related government news
GETNETWISE	www.getnetwise.org	Child online protection organization	Resource for families and caregivers to help kids have safe, educational, and entertaining online experiences; includes a glossary of terms, a guide to online safety, directions for reporting online trouble, a directory of online safety tools, and a listing great sites for kids to visit
HUSH COMMUNICAT-IONS	www.hush.com	Enhancement technology organization	Develops and distributes encryption technology to provide Internet users with secure Internet communications worldwide; allows users to protect the privacy of their e-mail and Web site traffic
INTERNET FRAUD WATCH	www.fraud.org	Fraud and identity theft organization	Provides tips, articles, bulletins, and other information on how to avoid fraud, protect your privacy, and safely surf the Internet.

ORGANIZATION	WEBSITE	FUNCTION	SERVICES
JUNKBUSTERS	www.junkbusters.com	Junk mail oversight organization	Site includes an array of information, resources, and publication links as well as actionable tips and online tools to help the consumer eliminate junk e-mail, telemarketing calls, and other kinds of unwanted solicitations
KIDZ PRIVACY SITE	www.ftc.gov/bcp/online/ edcams/kidzprivacy/ index.html	Child online protection organization	FTC site that offers guidance to parents, children and website operators on the dos and don'ts of children's online privacy
LUMERIA	www.lumeria.com	Privacy enhancement technology organization	Allows people to organize, securely access, and selectively share their information from any personal electronic device or computer that is connected to the net
MAILSHELL	www.mamilshell.com	Junk mail oversight organization	Offers advanced filtering technology against spam combined with more personalization, control, and privacy than any other service
MEDIA AWARENESS NETWORK	www.media-awareness.ca	Online resource for parents, educators and youth	Includes an interactive children's game on safe surfing
NATIONAL FRAUD INFORMATION CENTER (NFIC)	www.fraud.org	Advocacy organization	Nationwide toll-free hotline for advice on telephone solicitations and how to report telemarketing fraud; provides tips, articles, bulletins, and other information on how to avoid fraud, protect your privacy, and safely surf the Internet

ORGANIZATION	WEBSITE	FUNCTION	SERVICES
NATIONAL TELECOMMUNI-CATIONS AND INFORMATION ADMINISTRA-TION (NTIA)	www.ntia.doc.gov	Government organization	Primary source for domestic and international telecommunications and information technology issues including the federal Privacy Protection Acts; includes a listing of links to a range of privacy-related institutions and organizations
NETCOALITION	www.entcoalition.com	Trade organization	Brings together many of the world's leading Internet companies and serves as a unified public policy voice on Internet issues
ONLINE PRIVACY ALLIANCE	www.privacyalliance.org	Trade organization	A diverse group of corporations and associations who have come together to introduce and promote business-wide actions that create an environment of trust and foster the protection of individuals' privacy online
ONLINE PUBLIC EDUCATION NETWORK (OPEN)	www.internetalliance.org/ project/open/about.html	Child online protection organization	Offers downloadable opt-out forms, links to companies that allow you to opt-out online, and overview of specific business practices such as those of portals and online profilers
PRIVACY RIGHTS CLEARING-HOUSE (PRC)	www.privacyrights.org	Advocacy organization	Provides in-depth information on a broad range of privacy issues
PRIVACYX	www.privacyx.com	Privacy enhancement technology organization	Helps Internet users take control of their online privacy; offers free anonymous encrypted e-mail service that allows users to send and receive e-mail with complete privacy and security

ORGANIZATION	WEBSITE	FUNCTION	SERVICES
PRIVASEEK	www.privaseek.com	Privacy enhancement technology organization	Designs, builds, and manages systems and services that bring businesses and consumers together in a mutually beneficial, permission-based environment; developed a control tool that enables consumers to automatically safeguard and gain value from the use of personal information; acts as a buffer between consumers and websites, allowing users to decide which information can be shared and allows consumer to store that information for safe and secure online use
RESOURCES FOR INTERNET PARENTS	www.netparents.org	Child online protection organization	Provides information on parental control software
SPAMEX	www.spamex.com	Junk mail oversight organization	Disposable e-mail address service allows users to identify the sources of spam mail and stop the non-permission use of their e-mail addresses
TRANSUNION CORPORATION	www.tuc.com	Credit reporting organization	One of the three major national credit reporting agencies where the consumer can order a copy of their credit report online; read fraud FAQs; find out how to report credit card misuse or remove their name from pre-approved credit card offer mailing lists; find information on credit card scams, and the Marketing List Opt-Out section which tells how to delete one's name from junk mail lists

ORGANIZATION	WEBSITE	FUNCTION	SERVICES
TRUSTe Organization	www.truste.org	Online oversight organization	Offers the latest advice and information about online privacy and awards seals to responsible websites that meet stringent privacy policy requirements and enforcement criteria
U.S. CONSUMER GATEWAY	www.consumer.gov	Government organization	Provides a wide variety of federal information resources online; devoted to privacy and offers guidance on how to prohibit companies from using one's credit records for direct marketing and name from direct-mail and telemarketing lists
WIRED KIDS	www.wiredkids.org	Child online protection organization	Official North American site of UNESCO's Innocence in Danger program; mission is to allow children to enjoy the vast benefits of the Internet while at the same time protecting them from cybercriminals
ZERO-KNOWLEDGE SYSTEMS	www.zeroknowledge.com	Privacy enhancement technology organization	Designs tools and strategies to protect the privacy of Internet users; creates simple, easy-to-use software and services that integrate advanced mathematics, cryptography and source code

SOURCE: TRUSTe Organization.

APPENDIX 7:
THE CAN-SPAM ACT OF 2003—SELECTED PROVISIONS
[PUB. L. NO. 108-187, 12/16/03]

PUBLIC LAW 108-187 OF 2003, 108TH CONGRESS

SECTION 1. SHORT TITLE.

This Act may be cited as the 'Controlling the Assault of Non-Solicited Pornography and Marketing Act of 2003,' or the 'CAN-SPAM Act of 2003.'

***

SEC. 4. PROHIBITION AGAINST PREDATORY AND ABUSIVE COMMERCIAL E-MAIL.

(a) OFFENSE—

(1) IN GENERAL—Chapter 47 of title 18, United States Code, is amended by adding at the end the following new section:

'Sec. 1037. Fraud and related activity in connection with electronic mail

'(a) IN GENERAL—Whoever, in or affecting interstate or foreign commerce, knowingly—

'(1) accesses a protected computer without authorization, and intentionally initiates the transmission of multiple commercial electronic mail messages from or through such computer,

'(2) uses a protected computer to relay or retransmit multiple commercial electronic mail messages, with the intent to deceive or mislead recipients, or any Internet access service, as to the origin of such messages,

'(3) materially falsifies header information in multiple commercial electronic mail messages and intentionally initiates the transmission of such messages,

'(4) registers, using information that materially falsifies the identity of the actual registrant, for five or more electronic mai accounts or online user accounts or two or more domain names, and intentionally initiates the transmission of multiple commercial electronic mail messages from any combination of such accounts or domain names, or

'(5) falsely represents oneself to be the registrant or the legitimate successor in interest to the registrant of 5 or more Internet Protocol addresses, and intentionally initiates the transmission of multiple commercial electronic mail messages from such addresses, or conspires to do so, shall be punished as provided in subsection (b).

'(b) PENALTIES—The punishment for an offense under subsection (a) is—

'(1) a fine under this title, imprisonment for not more than 5 years, or both, if—

'(A) the offense is committed in furtherance of any felony under the laws of the United States or of any State; or

'(B) the defendant has previously been convicted under this section or section 1030, or under the law of any State for conduct involving the transmission of multiple commercial electronic mail messages or unauthorized access to a computer system;

'(2) a fine under this title, imprisonment for not more than 3 years, or both, if—

'(A) the offense is an offense under subsection (a)(1);

'(B) the offense is an offense under subsection (a)(4) and involved 20 or more falsified electronic mail or online user account registrations, or 10 or more falsified domain name registrations;

'(C) the volume of electronic mail messages transmitted in furtherance of the offense exceeded 2,500 during any 24-hour period, 25,000 during any 30-day period, or 250,000 during any 1-year period;

'(D) the offense caused loss to one or more persons aggregating $5,000 or more in value during any 1-year period;

'(E) as a result of the offense any individual committing the offense obtained anything of value aggregating $5,000 or more during any 1-year period; or

'(F) the offense was undertaken by the defendant in concert with three or more other persons with respect to whom the defendant occupied a position of organizer or leader; and

'(3) a fine under this title or imprisonment for not more than 1 year, or both, in any other case.

'(c) FORFEITURE—

'(1) IN GENERAL—The court, in imposing sentence on a person who is convicted of an offense under this section, shall order that the defendant forfeit to the United States—

'(A) any property, real or personal, constituting or traceable to gross proceeds obtained from such offense; and

'(B) any equipment, software, or other technology used or intended to be used to commit or to facilitate the commission of such offense.

'(2) PROCEDURES—The procedures set forth in section 413 of the Controlled Substances Act (21 U.S.C. § 853), other than subsection (d) of that section, and in Rule 32.2 of the Federal Rules of Criminal Procedure, shall apply to all stages of a criminal forfeiture proceeding under this section.

'(d) DEFINITIONS—In this section:

'(1) LOSS—The term 'loss' has the meaning given that term in section 1030(e) of this title.

'(2) MATERIALLY—For purposes of paragraphs (3) and (4) of subsection (a), header information or registration information is materially falsified if it is altered or concealed in a manner that would impair the ability of a recipient of the message, an Internet access service processing the message on behalf of a recipient, a person alleging a violation of this section, or a law enforcement agency to identify, locate, or respond to a person who initiated the electronic mail message or to investigate the alleged violation.

'(3) MULTIPLE—The term 'multiple' means more than 100 electronic mail messages during a 24-hour period, more than 1,000 electronic mail messages during a 30-day period, or more than 10,000 electronic mail messages during a 1-year period.

'(4) OTHER TERMS—Any other term has the meaning given that term by section 3 of the CAN-SPAM Act of 2003.'

(2) CONFORMING AMENDMENT—The chapter analysis for chapter 47 of title 18, United States Code, is amended by adding at the end the following:

'Sec. '1037. Fraud and related activity in connection with electronic mail..'

(b) UNITED STATES SENTENCING COMMISSION—

(1) DIRECTIVE—Pursuant to its authority under section 994(p) of title 28, United States Code, and in accordance with this section, the United States Sentencing Commission shall review and, as appropriate, amend the sentencing guidelines and policy statements to provide appropriate penalties for violations of section 1037 of title 18, United States Code, as added by this section, and other offenses that may be facilitated by the sending of large quantities of unsolicited electronic mail.

(2) REQUIREMENTS—In carrying out this subsection, the Sentencing Commission shall consider providing sentencing enhancements for—

(A) those convicted under section 1037 of title 18, United States Code, who—

(i) obtained electronic mail addresses through improper means, including—

(I) harvesting electronic mail addresses of the users of a website, proprietary service, or other online public forum operated by another person, without the authorization of such person; and

(II) randomly generating electronic mail addresses by computer; or

(ii) knew that the commercial electronic mail messages involved in the offense contained or advertised an Internet domain for which the registrant of the domain had provided false registration information; and

(B) those convicted of other offenses, including offenses involving fraud, identity theft, obscenity, child pornography, and the sexual exploitation of children, if such offenses involved the sending of large quantities of electronic mail.

(c) SENSE OF CONGRESS—It is the sense of Congress that—

(1) Spam has become the method of choice for those who distribute pornography, perpetrate fraudulent schemes, and introduce viruses, worms, and Trojan horses into personal and business computer systems; and

(2) the Department of Justice should use all existing law enforcement tools to investigate and prosecute those who send bulk commercial e-mail to facilitate the commission of Federal crimes, including the tools contained in chapters 47 and 63 of title 18, United States Code (relating to fraud and false statements); chapter 71 of title 18, United States Code (relating to obscenity); chapter 110 of title 18, United States Code (relating to the sexual exploitation of children); and chapter 95 of title 18, United States Code (relating to racketeering), as appropriate.

SEC. 5. OTHER PROTECTIONS FOR USERS OF COMMERCIAL ELECTRONIC MAIL.

(a) REQUIREMENTS FOR TRANSMISSION OF MESSAGES—

(1) PROHIBITION OF FALSE OR MISLEADING TRANSMISSION INFORMATION—

It is unlawful for any person to initiate the transmission, to a protected computer, of a commercial electronic mail message, or a transactional or relationship message, that contains, or is accompanied by, header information that is materially false or materially misleading. For purposes of this paragraph—

(A) header information that is technically accurate but includes an originating electronic mail address, domain name, or Internet

Protocol address the access to which for purposes of initiating the message was obtained by means of false or fraudulent pretenses or representations shall be considered materially misleading;

(B) a 'from' line (the line identifying or purporting to identify a person initiating the message) that accurately identifies any person who initiated the message shall not be considered materially false or materially misleading; and

(C) header information shall be considered materially misleading if it fails to identify accurately a protected computer used to initiate the message because the person initiating the message knowingly uses another protected computer to relay or retransmit the message for purposes of disguising its origin.

(2) PROHIBITION OF DECEPTIVE SUBJECT HEADINGS—

It is unlawful for any person to initiate the transmission to a protected computer of a commercial electronic mail message if such person has actual knowledge, or knowledge fairly implied on the basis of objective circumstances, that a subject heading of the message would be likely to mislead a recipient, acting reasonably under the circumstances, about a material fact regarding the contents or subject matter of the message (consistent with the criteria used in enforcement of section 5 of the Federal Trade Commission Act (15 U.S.C. § 45)).

(3) INCLUSION OF RETURN ADDRESS OR COMPARABLRE MECHANISM IN COMMERCIAL ELECTRONIC MAIL—

(A) IN GENERAL—It is unlawful for any person to initiate the transmission to a protected computer of a commercial electronic mail message that does not contain a functioning return electronic mail address or other Internet-based mechanism, clearly and conspicuously displayed, that—

(i) a recipient may use to submit, in a manner specified in the message, a reply electronic mail message or other form of Internet-based communication requesting not to receive future commercial electronic mail messages from that sender at the electronic mail address where the message was received; and

(ii) remains capable of receiving such messages or communications for no less than 30 days after the transmission of the original message.

(B) MORE DETAILED OPTIONS POSSIBLE—The person initiating a commercial electronic mail message may comply with subparagraph (A)(i) by providing the recipient a list or menu from which the recipient may choose the specific types of commercial electronic mail messages the recipient wants to receive or does not want to receive from the sender, if the list or menu includes an option under which the recipient may choose not to receive any commercial electronic mail messages from the sender.

(C) TEMPORARY INABILITY TO RECEIVE MESSAGES OR PROCESS REQUESTS—A return electronic mail address or other mechanism does not fail to satisfy the requirements of subparagraph (A) if it is unexpectedly and temporarily unable to receive messages or process requests due to a technical problem beyond the control of the sender if the problem is corrected within a reasonable time period.

(4) PROHIBITION OF TRANSMISSION OF COMMERCIAL ELECTRONIC MAIL AFTER OBJECTION—

(A) IN GENERAL—If a recipient makes a request using a mechanism provided pursuant to paragraph (3) not to receive some or any commercial electronic mail messages from such sender, then it is unlawful—

(i) for the sender to initiate the transmission to the recipient, more than 10 business days after the receipt of such request, of a commercial electronic mail message that falls within the scope of the request;

(ii) for any person acting on behalf of the sender to initiate the transmission to the recipient, more than 10 business days after the receipt of such request, of a commercial electronic mail message with actual knowledge, or knowledge fairly implied on the basis of objective circumstances, that such message falls within the scope of the request;

(iii) for any person acting on behalf of the sender to assist in initiating the transmission to the recipient, through the provision or selection of addresses to which the message will be sent, of a commercial electronic mail message with actual knowledge, or knowledge fairly implied on the basis of objective circumstances, that such message would violate clause (i) or (ii); or

(iv) for the sender, or any other person who knows that the recipient has made such a request, to sell, lease, exchange, or otherwise transfer or release the electronic mail address of the recipient (including through any transaction or other transfer involving mailing lists bearing the electronic mail address of the recipient) for any purpose other than compliance with this Act or other provision of law.

(B) SUBSEQUENT AFFIRMATIVE CONSENT—A prohibition in subparagraph (A) does not apply if there is affirmative consent by the recipient subsequent to the request under subparagraph (A).

(5) INCLUSION OF IDENTIFIER, OPT-OUT, AND PHYSICAL ADDRESS IN COMMERCIAL ELECTRONIC MAIL—

(A) It is unlawful for any person to initiate the transmission of any commercial electronic mail message to a protected computer unless the message provides—

(i) clear and conspicuous identification that the message is an advertisement or solicitation;

(ii) clear and conspicuous notice of the opportunity under paragraph (3) to decline to receive further commercial electronic mail messages from the sender; and

(iii) a valid physical postal address of the sender.

(B) Subparagraph (A)(i) does not apply to the transmission of a commercial electronic mail message if the recipient has given prior affirmative consent to receipt of the message.

(6) MATERIALLY—For purposes of paragraph (1), the term 'materially,' when used with respect to false or misleading header information, includes the alteration or concealment of header information in a manner that would impair the ability of an Internet access service processing the message on behalf of a recipient, a person alleging a violation of this section, or a law enforcement agency to identify, locate, or respond to a person who initiated the electronic mail message or to investigate the alleged violation, or the ability of a recipient of the message to respond to a person who initiated the electronic message.

(b) AGGRAVATED VIOLATIONS RELATING TO COMMERCIAL ELECTRONIC MAIL—

(1) ADDRESS HARVESTING AND DICTIONARY ATTACKS—

(A) IN GENERAL—It is unlawful for any person to initiate the transmission, to a protected computer, of a commercial electronic mail message that is unlawful under subsection (a), or to assist in the origination of such message through the provision or selection of addresses to which the message will be transmitted, if such person had actual knowledge, or knowledge fairly implied on the basis of objective circumstances, that—

(i) the electronic mail address of the recipient was obtained using an automated means from an Internet website or proprietary online service operated by another person, and such website or online service included, at the time the address was obtained, a notice stating that the operator of such website or online service will not give, sell, or otherwise transfer addresses maintained by such website or online service to any other party for the purposes of initiating, or enabling others to initiate, electronic mail messages; or

(ii) the electronic mail address of the recipient was obtained using an automated means that generates possible electronic mail addresses by combining names, letters, or numbers into numerous permutations.

(B) DISCLAIMER—Nothing in this paragraph creates an ownership or proprietary interest in such electronic mail addresses.

(2) AUTOMATED CREATION OF MULTIPLE ELECTRONIC MAIL ACCOUNTS—

It is unlawful for any person to use scripts or other automated means to register for multiple electronic mail accounts or online user accounts from which to transmit to a protected computer, or enable another person to transmit to a protected computer, a commercial electronic mail message that is unlawful under subsection (a).

(3) RELAY OR RETRANSMISSION THROUGH UNAUTHORIZED ACCESS—

It is unlawful for any person knowingly to relay or retransmit a commercial electronic mail message that is unlawful under subsection (a) from a protected computer or computer network that such person has accessed without authorization.

(c) SUPPLEMENTARY RULEMAKING AUTHORITY—The Commission shall by regulation, pursuant to section 13—

(1) modify the 10-business-day period under subsection (a)(4)(A) or subsection (a)(4)(B), or both, if the Commission determines that a different period would be more reasonable after taking into account—

(A) the purposes of subsection (a);

(B) the interests of recipients of commercial electronic mail; and

(C) the burdens imposed on senders of lawful commercial electronic mail; and

(2) specify additional activities or practices to which subsection (b) applies if the Commission determines that those activities or practices are contributing substantially to the proliferation of commercial electronic mail messages that are unlawful under subsection (a).

(d) REQUIREMENT TO PLACE WARNING LABELS ON COMMERCIAL ELECTRONIC MAIL CONTAINING SEXUALLY ORIENTED MATERIAL—

(1) IN GENERAL—No person may initiate in or affecting interstate commerce the transmission, to a protected computer, of any commercial electronic mail message that includes sexually oriented material and—

(A) fail to include in subject heading for the electronic mail message the marks or notices prescribed by the Commission under this subsection; or

(B) fail to provide that the matter in the message that is initially viewable to the recipient, when the message is opened by any recipient and absent any further actions by the recipient, includes only—

(i) to the extent required or authorized pursuant to paragraph (2), any such marks or notices;

(ii) the information required to be included in the message pursuant to subsection (a)(5); and

(iii) instructions on how to access, or a mechanism to access, the sexually oriented material.

(2) PRIOR AFFIRMATIVE CONSENT—Paragraph (1) does not apply to the transmission of an electronic mail message if the recipient has given prior affirmative consent to receipt of the message.

(3) PRESCRIPTION OF MARKS AND NOTICES—Not later than 120 days after the date of the enactment of this Act, the Commission in consultation with the Attorney General shall prescribe clearly identifiable marks or notices to be included in or associated with commercial electronic mail that contains sexually oriented material, in order to inform the recipient of that fact and to facilitate filtering of such electronic mail. The Commission shall publish in the Federal Register and provide notice to the public of the marks or notices prescribed under this paragraph.

(4) DEFINITION—

In this subsection, the term 'sexually oriented material' means any material that depicts sexually explicit conduct (as that term is defined in section 2256 of title 18, United States Code), unless the depiction constitutes a small and insignificant part of the whole, the remainder of which is not primarily devoted to sexual matters.

(5) PENALTY—

Whoever knowingly violates paragraph (1) shall be fined under title 18, United States Code, or imprisoned not more than 5 years, or both.

***

SEC. 8. EFFECT ON OTHER LAWS.

(a) FEDERAL LAW—(1) Nothing in this Act shall be construed to impair the enforcement of section 223 or 231 of the Communications Act of 1934 (47 U.S.C. § 223 or 231, respectively), chapter 71 (relating to obscenity) or 110 (relating to sexual exploitation of children) of title 18, United States Code, or any other Federal criminal statute.

(2) Nothing in this Act shall be construed to affect in any way the Commission's authority to bring enforcement actions under FTC Act for materially false or deceptive representations or unfair practices in commercial electronic mail messages.

(b) STATE LAW—

(1) IN GENERAL—This Act supersedes any statute, regulation, or rule of a State or political subdivision of a State that expressly regulates the use of electronic mail to send commercial messages, except to the extent that any such statute, regulation, or rule prohibits falsity or deception in any portion of a commercial electronic mail message or information attached thereto.

(2) STATE LAW NOT SPECIFIC TO ELECTRONIC MAIL—This Act shall not be construed to preempt the applicability of—

(A) State laws that are not specific to electronic mail, including State trespass, contract, or tort law; or

(B) other State laws to the extent that those laws relate to acts of fraud or computer crime.

(c) NO EFFECT ON POLICIES OF PROVIDERS OF INTERNET ACCESS SERVICE—

Nothing in this Act shall be construed to have any effect on the lawfulness or unlawfulness, under any other provision of law, of the adoption, implementation, or enforcement by a provider of Internet access service of a policy of declining to transmit, route, relay, handle, or store certain types of electronic mail messages.

SEC. 9. DO-NOT-E-MAIL REGISTRY.

(a) IN GENERAL—Not later than 6 months after the date of enactment of this Act, the Commission shall transmit to the Senate Committee on Commerce, Science, and Transportation and the House of Representatives Committee on Energy and Commerce a report that—

(1) sets forth a plan and timetable for establishing a nationwide marketing Do-Not-E-Mail registry;

(2) includes an explanation of any practical, technical, security, privacy, enforceability, or other concerns that the Commission has regarding such a registry; and

(3) includes an explanation of how the registry would be applied with respect to children with e-mail accounts.

APPENDIX 8:
DIRECTORY OF STATE CONSUMER PROTECTION AGENCIES

STATE	ADDRESS	TELEPHONE FAX	E-MAIL	WEBSITE
ALABAMA	Office of the Attorney General Consumer Protection Division 11 S. Union Street Montgomery, AL 36130	334-242-7335 None listed	none listed	www.ago.state.al.us/
ALASKA	Office of the Attorney General Consumer Protection Section 1031 W. 4th Ave., Suite 200 Anchorage, AK 99501	907-269-5100 907-276-8554	none listed	www.law.state.ak.us/
ARIZONA	Office of the Attorney General Financial Fraud Division 1275 W. Washington St. Phoenix, AZ 85007	602-542-5025 602-542-4085	none listed	www.azag.gov/

STATE	ADDRESS	TELEPHONE FAX	E-MAIL	WEBSITE
ARKANSAS	Office of the Attorney General Consumer Protection Division 323 Center St., Suite 200 Little Rock, AR 72201	501-682-2007 501-682-8118	consumer@ag.state.ar.us	www.ag.state.ar.us/
CALIFORNIA	Department of Consumer Affairs 1625 North Market Blvd. Sacrament, CA 95834	916-445-1254 none listed	dca@dca.gov	www.dca.ca.gov/
COLORADO	Office of the Attorney General Consumer Protection Division 1525 Sherman St., 5th Floor Denver, CO 80203	303-866-5079 303-866-5443	none listed	none listed
CONNECTICUT	Department of Consumer Protection 165 Capitol Ave. Hartford, CT 06106	860-713-7243	none listed	www.ct.gov/dcp/
DELAWARE	Office of the Attorney General Fraud and Consumer Protection Division 820 N. French St. Wilmington, DE 19801	302-577-8600 302-577-2496	attorney.general@state.de.us	www.state.de.us/attgen/
DISTRICT OF COLUMBIA	Department of Consumer & Regulatory Affairs 941 North Capitol St. NE Washington, DC 20002	202-442-4400 202-442-9445	dcra@dc.gov	www.dcra.dc.gov/

STATE	ADDRESS	TELEPHONE FAX	E-MAIL	WEBSITE
FLORIDA	Office of the Attorney General Economic Crimes Unit PL-01 The Capitol Tallahassee, FL 32399	850-414-3600 850-488-4483	none listed	www.myfloridalegal.com/
GEORGIA	Governor's Office of Consumer Affairs 2 Martin Luther King Jr. Dr. Suite 356 Atlanta, GA 30334	404-656-3790 404-651-9018	none listed	www.consumer.georgia.gov
HAWAII	Office of Consumer Protection 235 South Beretania St. Room 801 Honolulu, HI 96813	808-586-2636 none listed	none listed	www.hawaii.gov/dcca/ocp/
IDAHO	Office of the Attorney General Consumer Protection Unit 650 West State St. Boise, ID 83720	208-334-2424 208-334-2850	none listed	www.state.id.us/ag/
ILLINOIS	Office of the Attorney General Consumer Fraud Bureau 100 West Randolph, 12th Floor Chicago, IL 60601	312-814-3374 312-814-2593	ag_consumer@atg.state.il.us	www.illinoisattorneygeneral.gov/
INDIANA	Office of the Attorney General Consumer Protection Division 302 West Washington St. Indianapolis, IN 46204	317-232-6201 317-232-7979	none listed	www.in.gov/attorneygeneral/

STATE	ADDRESS	TELEPHONE FAX	E-MAIL	WEBSITE
IOWA	Office of the Attorney General Consumer Protection Division 1305 East Walnut St., 2nd Floor Des Moines, IA 50319	515-281-5926 515-281-6771	consumer@ag.state.ia.us	www.iowaattorneygeneral.org/
KANSAS	Office of the Attorney General Consumer Protection Division 120 S.W. 10th, 2nd Floor Topeka, KS 66612	785-296-3751 785-291-3699	cprotect@ksag.org	www.ksag.org/
KENTUCKY	Office of the Attorney General Consumer Protection Division 1024 Capital Center Dr. Suite 200 Frankfort, KY 40601	502-696-5389 502-573-8317	Attorney.general@ag.ky.gov	www.ag.ky.gov/
LOUISIANA	Office of the Attorney General Consumer Protection Division P.O. Box 94005 Baton Rouge, LA 70804	800-351-4889 225-326-6499	none listed	www.ag.state.la.us/
MAINE	Office of the Attorney General Consumer Protection Division 6 State House Station Augusta, ME 04333	207-626-8800 207-626-8812	Consumer.mediation@ state.me.us	www.maine.gov/
MARYLAND	Office of the Attorney General Consumer Protection Division 200 Saint Paul Place, 16th Floor Baltimore, MD 21202	410-576-6550 410-576-7040	consumer@oag.state.md.us	www.oag.state.md.us/consumer/

STATE	ADDRESS	TELEPHONE FAX	E-MAIL	WEBSITE
MASSACHUSETTS	Office of the Attorney General Consumer Protection Division One Ashburton Place Boston, MA 02108	617-727-8400 617-727-3265	none listed	www.mass.gov/ago/
MICHIGAN	Office of the Attorney General Consumer Protection Division P.O. Box 30213 Lansing, MI 48909	517-373-1140 517-241-3771	none listed	www.michigan.gov/ag/
MINNESOTA	Office of the Attorney General Consumer Services Division 445 Minnesota St. St. Paul, MN 55101	651-296-3353 651-282-2155	attorney.general@state.mn.us	www.ag.state.mn.us/consumer/
MISSISSIPPI	Office of the Attorney General Consumer Protection Division P.O. Box 22947 Jackson, MS 39225	601-359-4230 601-359-4231	none listed	www.ago.state.ms.us/
MISSOURI	Office of the Attorney General Consumer Protection Division 207 W. High St. Jefferson City, MO 65102	573-751-3321 573-751-0774	attgenmail@moago.org	www.ago.mo.gov/
MONTANA	Office of Consumer Protection 1219 8th Avenue Helena, MT 59620	406-444-4500 406-444-9860	none listed	www.mt.gov/consumer/
NEBRASKA	Office of the Attorney General 2115 State Capitol Lincoln, NE 68509	402-471-2682 402-271-0006	none listed	www.ago.state.ne.us/

STATE	ADDRESS	TELEPHONE FAX	E-MAIL	WEBSITE
NEVADA	Consumer Affairs Division 1850 East Sahara Ave. Suite 101 Las Vegas, NV 89104	702-486-7355 702-486-7371	ncad@fyiconsumer.org	www.fyiconsumer.org
NEW HAMPSHIRE	Consumer Protection Bureau 33 Capitol St. Concord, NH 03301	603-271-3641 603-223-6202	none listed	www.doj.nh.gov/consumer/index.html/
NEW JERSEY	Division of Consumer Affairs P.O. Box 45027 Newark, NJ 07101	973-504-6200 973-648-3538	askconsumeraffairs@ lps.state.nj.us	www.state.nj.us/lps/ca/home.htm/
NEW MEXICO	Office of the Attorney General Consumer Protection Division 407 Galisteo Santa Fe, NM 87504	505-827-6060 505-827-6685	none listed	www.ago.state.nm.us/
NEW YORK	Consumer Protection Board 5 Empire State Plaza Suite 2102 Albany, NY 12223	518-474-8583 518-474-2474	webmaster@consumer.state.ny.us	www.nysconsumer.gov/
NORTH CAROLINA	Consumer Protection Division 9002 Mail Service Center Raleigh, NC 27699	919-716-6000 919-716-6050	none listed	www.ncdoj.com/
NORTH DAKOTA	Office of the Attorney General Consumer Protection Division 600 E. Boulevard Ave. Dept.125 Bismarck, ND 58505	701-328-3404 none listed	cppat@state.nd.us	www.ag.state.nd.us/

STATE	ADDRESS	TELEPHONE FAX	E-MAIL	WEBSITE
OHIO	Office of the Attorney General Consumer Protection Section 30 East Broad St., 17th Floor Columbus, OH 43215	614-466-4320 614-728-7583	consumer@ag.state.oh.us	www.ag.state.oh.us/
OKLAHOMA	Office of the Attorney General Consumer Protection Unit 313 NE 21st Street Oklahoma City, OK 73105	405-521-2029 405-528-1867	none listed	www.oag.state.ok.us/
OREGON	Consumer Protection Section 1162 Court St. NE Salem, OR 97310	503-947-4333 503-378-5017	none listed	www.doj.state.or.us/
PENNSYLVANIA	Office of the Attorney General Bureau of Consumer Protection Strawberry Square, 16th floor Harrisburg, PA 17120	717-787-3391 717-787-8242	none listed	www.attorenygeneral.gov/
RHODE ISLAND	Office of the Attorney General Consumer Protection Unit 150 South Main St. Providence, RI 02903	401-274-4400 401-222-5110	none listed	www.riag.state.ri.us/
SOUTH CAROLINA	Department of Consumer Affairs 3600 Forest Drive, Suite 300 Columbia, SC 29250	803-734-4200 803-734-4286	scdca@dca.state.sc.us	www.scconsumer.ov/
SOUTH DAKOTA	Office of the Attorney General Department of Consumer Affairs 1302 E. Hwy 14, Suite 3 Pierre, SD 57501	605-773-4400 605-773-7163	consumerhelp@state.sd.us	www.state.sd.us/atg/

STATE	ADDRESS	TELEPHONE FAX	E-MAIL	WEBSITE
TENNESSEE	Division of Consumer Affairs 500 James Robertson Parkway 5th Floor Nashville, TN 37243	615-741-4737 615-532-4994	consumeraffairs@state.tn.us	www.state.tn.us/consumer/
TEXAS	Office of the Attorney General Consumer Protection Division P.O. Box 12548 Austin, TX 78711	512-463-2100 512-473-8301	cac@oag.state.tx.us	www.oag.state.tx.us/
UTAH	Office of the Attorney General Consumer Protection Division 160 East 300 South Salt Lake City, UT 84114	801-530-6601 801-530-6001	consumerprotection@utah.gov	www.consumerprotection.utah.gov/
VERMONT	Office of the Attorney General Consumer Assistance Program 104 Morrill Hall, UVM Burlington, VT 05405	802-656-3183 802-656-1423	consumer@uvm.edu	www.atg.state.vt.us/
VIRGINIA	Office of the Attorney General Consumer Litigation Section 900 East Main St. Richmond, VA 23219	804-786-2116 804-786-0122	mail@oag.state.va.us	www.oag.state.va.us/
WASHINGTON	Office of the Attorney General Regional Consumer Resource Center 1125 Washington St. SE Olympia, WA 98504	800-551-4636 none listed	none listed	www.atg.wa.gov/

STATE	ADDRESS	TELEPHONE FAX	E-MAIL	WEBSITE
WEST VIRGINIA	Office of the Attorney General Consumer Protection Division 812 Quarrier St., 6th Floor Charleston, WV 25326	304-558-8986 304-558-0184	consumer@wvago.gov	www.wvago.us/
WISCONSIN	Department of Consumer Protection 2811 Agriculture Dr. Madison, WI 53708	608-224-4949 608-224-4939	hotline@datcp.state.wi.us	www.datcp.state.wi.us/
WYOMING	Office of the Attorney General Consumer Protection Unit 123 State Capitol 200 W. 24th St. Cheyenne, WY 82002	307-777-7841 307-777-6869	agwebmaster@state.wy.us	Attorneygeneral.state.wy.us/

SOURCE: The Federal Citizen Information Center, U.S. General Services Administration.

APPENDIX 9: SAMPLE INTERNET PRIVACY STATEMENT OUTLINE

PART A—IDENTIFY THE WEBSITE ADMINISTRATOR

1. This is the Web site of [Company Name].

2. Our postal address is [Address].

3. We can be reached via e-mail at [e-mail address].

4. We can be reached by telephone at [telephone number].

PART B—FOR EACH VISITOR TO OUR WEB PAGE, OUR WEB SERVER AUTOMATICALLY RECOGNIZES (CHOOSE ONE):

1. The consumer's domain name and e-mail address (where possible);

2. Only the consumer's domain name, but not the e-mail address (where possible);

3. No information regarding the domain or e-mail address; or

4. Other [please explain].

PART C—WE COLLECT (CHOOSE ALL THAT APPLY):

1. Only the domain name, but not the e-mail address of visitors to our Web page;

2. The domain name and e-mail address (where possible) of visitors to our Web page;

3. The e-mail addresses of those who post messages to our bulletin board;

4. The e-mail addresses of those who communicate with us via e-mail;

5. The e-mail addresses of those who make postings to our chat areas;

6. Aggregate information on what pages consumers access or visit;

7. User-specific information on what pages consumers access or visit;

8. Information volunteered by the consumer, such as survey information and/or site registrations;

9. No information on consumers who browse our Web page; and/or

10. Other [please explain].

PART D—THE INFORMATION WE COLLECT IS (CHOOSE ALL THAT APPLY):

1. Used for internal review and is then discarded;

2. Used to improve the content of our Web page;

3. Used to customize the content and/or layout of our page for each individual visitor;

'4. Used to notify visitors about updates to our Web site;

5. Used by us to contact consumers for marketing purposes;

6. Shared with other reputable organizations to help them contact consumers for marketing purposes;

7. Not shared with other organizations for commercial purposes; and/or

8. Other [please explain].

PART E—WITH RESPECT TO COOKIES:

1. We do not set any cookies; or

2. We use cookies to: (choose all that apply)

(a) Store visitors preferences;

(b) Record session information, such as items that consumers add to their shopping cart;

(c) Record user-specific information on what pages users access or visit;

(d) Alert visitors to new areas that we think might be of interest to them when they return to our site;

(e) To record past activity at a site in order to provide better service when visitors return to our site;

(f) Ensure that visitors are not repeatedly sent the same banner ads;

(g) Customize Web page content on visitors' browser type or other information that the visitor sends; and/or

(h) Other [please explain].

PART F—IF YOU DO NOT WANT TO RECEIVE E-MAIL FROM US IN THE FUTURE, PLEASE TELL US THAT YOU DO NOT WANT TO RECEIVE E-MAIL FROM OUR COMPANY AND PLEASE LET US KNOW BY (CHOOSE ALL THAT APPLY):

1. Sending us e-mail at the above address;

2. Calling us at the above telephone number;

3. Writing to us at the above address;

4. Visiting the following URL; and/or

5. Other [please explain].

PART G—FROM TIME TO TIME, WE MAKE THE E-MAIL ADDRESSES OF THOSE WHO ACCESS OUR SITE AVAILABLE TO OTHER REPUTABLE ORGANIZATIONS WHOSE PRODUCTS OR SERVICES WE THINK YOU MIGHT FIND INTERESTING. IF YOU DO NOT WANT US TO SHARE YOUR E-MAIL ADDRESS WITH OTHER COMPANIES OR ORGANIZATIONS, PLEASE TELL US THAT YOU DO NOT WANT US TO SHARE YOUR E-MAIL ADDRESS WITH OTHER COMPANIES, AND LET US KNOW BY (CHOOSE ALL THAT APPLY):

1. Sending us e-mail at the above address;

2. Calling us at the above telephone number;

3. Writing to us at the above address;

4. Visiting the following URL; and/or

5. Other (please explain).

PART H—FROM TIME TO TIME, WE MAKE OUR CUSTOMER E-MAIL LIST AVAILABLE TO OTHER REPUTABLE ORGANIZATIONS WHOSE PRODUCTS OR SERVICES WE THINK YOU MIGHT FIND INTERESTING. IF YOU DO NOT WANT US TO SHARE YOUR E-MAIL ADDRESS WITH OTHER COMPANIES OR ORGANIZATIONS, PLEASE LET US KNOW BY (CHOOSE ALL THAT APPLY):

1. Sending us e-mail at the above address;

2. Calling us at the above telephone number;

3. Writing to us at the above address;

4. Visiting the following URL; and/or

5. Other (please explain).

PART I—IF YOU SUPPLY US WITH YOUR POSTAL ADDRESS ONLINE (CHOOSE EITHER OPTION 1 OR A COMBINATION OF OPTIONS 2 AND 3):

1. You will only receive the information for which you provided us your address;

2. You may receive periodic mailings from us with information on new products and services or upcoming events. If you do not wish to receive such mailings, please let us know by (choose all that apply):

(a) Sending us e-mail at the above address;

(b) Calling us at the above telephone number;

(c) Writing to us at the above address;

(d) Visiting the following URL; and/or

(e) Other (please explain).

3. You may receive mailings from other reputable companies. You can, however, have your name put on our do-not-share list by (choose all that apply):

(a) Sending us e-mail at the above address;

(b) Calling us at the above telephone number;

(c) Writing to us at the above address;

(d) Visiting the following URL; and/or

(e) Other (please explain).

Please provide us with your exact name and address. We will be sure your name is removed from the list we share with other organizations.

PART J—PERSONS WHO SUPPLY US WITH THEIR TELEPHONE NUMBERS ONLINE (CHOOSE ALL THAT APPLY):

1. Will only receive telephone contact from us with information regarding orders they have placed online-; and/or

2. May receive telephone contact from us with information regarding new products and services or upcoming events. If you do not wish to receive such telephone calls, please let us know by (choose all that apply):

(a) Sending us e-mail at the above address;

(b) Calling us at the above telephone number;

(c) Writing to us at the above address;

(d) Visiting the following URL; and/or

(e) Other (please explain)

3. May receive telephone contact from other reputable companies. You can, however, have your name put on our do-not-share list by (choose all that apply):

(a) Sending us e-mail at the above address;

(b) Calling us at the above telephone number;

(c) Writing to us at the above address;

(d) Visiting the following URL; and/or

(e) Other (please explain)

Please provide us with your name and phone number. We will be sure your name is removed from the list we share with other organizations.

PART K—AD SERVERS (CHOOSE ONE):

1. We do not partner with or have special relationships with any ad server companies; or

2. To try and bring you offers that are of interest to you, we have relationships with other companies that we allow to place ads on our Web pages. As a result of your visit to our site, ad server companies may collect information such as your domain type, your IP address, and clickstream information. For further information, consult the privacy policies of: [List the URLs for the privacy statements of the ad server companies with whom you have contracted or partnered].

PART L—FROM TIME TO TIME, WE MAY USE CUSTOMER INFORMATION FOR NEW, UNANTICIPATED USES NOT PREVIOUSLY DISCLOSED IN OUR PRIVACY NOTICE. IF YOUR INFORMATION PRACTICES CHANGE AT SOME TIME IN THE FUTURE (CHOOSE ALL THAT APPLY):

1. We will contact you before we use your data for these new purposes to notify you of the policy change and to provide you with the ability to opt out of these new uses;

2. We will post the policy changes to our Web site to notify you of these changes and provide you with the ability to opt out of these new uses. If you are concerned about how your information is used, you should check back at our Web site periodically;

3. We will use for these new purposes only data collected from the time of the policy change forward;

4. Customers may prevent their information from being used for purposes other than those for which it was originally collected by:

5. Sending us e-mail at the above address;

6. Calling us at the above telephone number;

7. Writing to us at the above address;

8. Visiting the following URL; or

9. Other (please explain).

PART M—UPON REQUEST, WE PROVIDE SITE VISITORS ACCESS TO (CHOOSE ALL THAT APPLY):

1. All information [including proprietary information] that we maintain about them;

2. Financial information (e.g., credit card account information) that we maintain about them;

3. Unique identifier information (e.g., customer number or password) that we maintain about them;

4. Transaction information (e.g., dates on which customers made purchases, amounts and types of purchases) that we maintain about them;

5. Communications that the consumer/visitor has directed to our site (e.g., e-mails, customer inquiries);

6. Contact information (e.g., name, address, phone number) that we maintain about them;

7. A description of information that we maintain about them;

8. No information that we have collected and that we maintain about them.

CONSUMERS CAN ACCESS THIS INFORMATION BY (CHOOSE ALL THAT APPLY):

1. Sending us e-mail at the above address;

2. Calling us at the above telephone number;

3. Writing to us at the above address;

4. Visiting the following URL; and/or

5. Other (please explain).

PART N—UPON REQUEST, WE OFFER VISITORS:

1. No ability to have factual inaccuracies corrected in information that we maintain about them; or

2. The ability to have inaccuracies corrected in: (choose all that apply)

3. Contact information;

4. Financial information;

5. Unique identifiers;

6. Transaction information;

7. Communications that the consumer/visitor has directed to the site; and/or

8. All information that we maintain.

CONSUMERS CAN HAVE THIS INFORMATION CORRECTED BY (CHOOSE ALL THAT APPLY):

1. Sending us e-mail at the above address;

2. Calling us at the above telephone number;

3. Writing to us at the above address;

4. Visiting the following URL; and/or

5. Other (please explain).

PART O—SECURITY (CHOOSE ALL THAT APPLY):

1. We always use industry-standard encryption technologies when transferring and receiving consumer data exchanged with our site;

2. When we transfer and receive certain types of sensitive information such as financial or health information, we redirect visitors to a secure server and will notify visitors through a pop-up screen on our site;

3. We have appropriate security measures in place in our physical facilities to protect against the loss, misuse, or alteration of information that we have collected from you at our site; and/or

4. Other (please explain).

PART P—ENFORCEMENT

1. If you feel that this site is not following its stated information policy, you may contact [Company Name] at the above addresses or phone number;

2. The Direct Marketing Association's Committee on Ethical Business Practices at [contact information];

3. State or local chapters of the Better Business Bureau;

4. State or local consumer protection office;

5. The Federal Trade Commission by telephone [202-FTC-HELP] or electronically [http://www.ftc.gov/]; and/or

6. Other [please explain].

SOURCE: The Direct Marketing Association.

APPENDIX 10:
THE AMERICAN EXPRESS INTERNET PRIVACY STATEMENT

At American Express, we value and protect your privacy. We thank you for the trust that you place in us and we want you to know that the information you share with us will be treated with care.

The objective of our Online Privacy Statement is to disclose and explain what information we collect, use, and share and to explain the privacy choices that you can make. We encourage you to read our Online Privacy Statement as well as those of all websites that you visit.

This American Express Online Privacy Statement applies only to our United States visitors to AmericanExpress.com.

Effective Date: August 31, 2006

WHAT INFORMATION WE COLLECT AND HOW WE USE IT

You should feel secure in knowing that American Express does not sell or share personal information with marketers outside of American Express for purposes of offering their own products or services.

Collecting Information About You

When you visit our website, we collect information in order to service your accounts, save you time and better respond to your needs. We use "cookie" technology to collect site statistical information and improve your customer experience. Cookies set by American Express do not capture any personally identifiable information, such as your individual e-mail address.

We automatically collect some statistical data as you browse this website. For example, we automatically collect your "IP address" used to connect your computer to the Internet, browser type and version, operating system and platform, average time spent on our site, pages viewed, information searched for, access times, "clickstream data," and other relevant information about your online experience.

You may browse our Website anonymously by choosing not to provide us with any "personally identifiable information (PII)," such as your name or e-mail address, or choosing not to register during your visits to our sites. When you browse this way, we will not link your online activity with the accounts you may have with us.

American Express may use "Web beacons" to present offers on americanexpress.com, other sites on which American Express advertises, or in our e-mails. This enables us to enhance e-mail offers and track website usage. We sometimes use "vendors" and "business partners" to manage web beacons and the data they collect; however, Web beacons do not capture your individual e-mail address or any other personal information that you enter on the American Express site.

Web beacons are sometimes used on AmericanExpress.com webpages where transactions take place. In addition, e-mail offers that we send may contain web beacons to help us record response rates and to assist us in measuring the offer's effectiveness. No personally identifiable information such as name, address, telephone number, credit card number, or e-mail address is ever collected or passed via the use of web beacons.

Using Your Personal Information

American Express does not sell or share customer information with entities outside of American Express who may want to market to you their own products and services. You don't need to take any action for this benefit. American Express uses your information to process applications, complete transactions, respond to your requests, deliver the products and services in which you enroll or for which you apply, and notify you of promotions, updates, or special offers that we think may interest you. We also use your information to provide you with a more effective customer experience while on our website. In order to do this, we may process your information or combine it with other information that is publicly available. This enables us to customize your American Express experience and provide you with more relevant offers. American Express may also use the information that we collect from you online to market to you through alternative channels.

American Express may share your information within our family of companies; and, to provide services to you, we may share information with carefully selected "vendors" and "business partners" with whom we work. This includes companies that manage accounts; offer affinity, frequent-user, and reward programs; and, companies that perform marketing services and other business operations for us. All companies that act on our behalf are contractually obligated to keep all information confidential and to use the customer information only to provide the services we ask them to perform for you and us.

If you apply for products and services online, we may share information we collect about you with credit bureaus and similar organizations if we have your express consent or when required or permitted by law. To the extent permitted by law, we may disclose personally identifiable information to government authorities or third parties pursuant to a legal request, subpoena, or other legal process. We may also use or disclose your information as permitted by law to perform charge verifications, report or collect debts owed, fight fraud, or protect the legal rights of American Express, our customers, our websites, or its users.

Using Your E-mail Address

We may use your e-mail address for the following types of e-mail messages:

• Occasional Updates and Valuable Offers. We may send you e-mail updates about our products and services as well as valuable offers from our business partners that we send you on their behalf. For examples of these offers, please visit American Express Selects.

• Regularly Scheduled E-mail Newsletters related to American Express products or services in which you are enrolled.

You can also elect to receive other types of e-mail messages from us, including newsletters, alerts, or notifications.

Please note that even if you opt-out of marketing e-mails, we will continue to send you e-mail service notifications that are related to your account(s). These include e-mails that provide account information, answer your questions about a product or service, facilitate or confirm a sale, or fulfill a legal or regulatory disclosure requirement.

Mobile Offers

American Express does not sell or share mobile phone numbers with third parties and will only use the information for the specific communication into which you have opted-in.

Ads That Link to Our Site

American Express hires other companies to place our banner ads on other websites and to perform tracking and reporting activities on this site and other websites. This enables us to learn which advertisements and websites bring users to our websites. A unique "cookie," if it exists on your computer, is placed there either by us, an ad management partner, or by another advertiser who works with our ad management partners. However, these companies do not collect personally identifiable information in this manner and we do not give any personally identifiable information to them.

Third-party ad partners have their own privacy policies. If you would like more information about their privacy policies, including information on how to opt-out of their tracking methods, please visit this link.

Children's Privacy

AmericanExpress.com is not intended for use by children. We do not knowingly solicit data online from, or market online to, children under the age of 13. If we obtain personally identifiable information in error on a child under the age of 13 is collected, we will delete that information from our systems.

COMMUNICATION CHOICES

American Express respects the choices that you make regarding your privacy. You may request that American Express no longer send you marketing e-mails. Marketing e-mails from American Express may include information about new products and services being offered. If you choose not to hear from us, you will not receive offers about American Express products and services that may be of value to you.

How To Opt-In or Opt-Out of E-mail Marketing Offers

At the American Express E-mail Marketing Preferences link, you can change your e-mail marketing preferences to opt-out of marketing offers from American Express.

If you have opted-in to receive certain marketing e-mails from American Express, but decide that you no longer wish to subscribe, please follow the instructions that are located at the bottom of those e-mail messages in order to opt-out.

Additional Opt-Out Methods—You may also opt-out of e-mail marketing by mail or telephone.

> **By Mail:**
> P.O. Box 299836
> Ft Lauderdale, FL 33329–9836

By Telephone:
Call (800) 297–8378 to opt-in or opt-out of American Express marketing offers.
American Express Card Members may also call the phone number listed on the back of your Card(s).

Access or Changes to Your Information Online

If you wish to make an adjustment to your online account, please use your User ID and Password to log-in on our homepage. You will then have access to your personal information and can correct or update your data.

SECURING YOUR INFORMATION

We take reasonable precautions to keep all information obtained from our online visitors secure against unauthorized access and use and we periodically review our security measures. When you voluntarily provide us with information while registering, such as your name, address phone number, or social security number, your information is encrypted and transferred over a secure connection, available on browsers such as Mozilla Firefox or Microsoft Internet Explorer. The padlock icon found in most browsers will appear locked and the first characters of the website address will change from "http" to "https" if you are accessing a secure server.

Do not use e-mail to send us any personally identifiable information, since it would be unencrypted and can be read by anyone who receives or intercepts it. You may, however, safely contact us online by using our Secure Message Center. Once your information reaches us, we store it behind a secure firewall that blocks access to the information from outside of our network. Only American Express authorized individuals are allowed to access the information.

At American Express, security is about protecting our employees, other team members, customers, and business and information resources. American Express uses appropriate security controls and processes to provide this protection. Everyone working on the American Express team is responsible for taking the actions required to ensure this and compliance with laws and regulations.

APPLICABILITY OF THE ONLINE PRIVACY STATEMENT

This American Express Online Privacy Statement applies only to United States visitors to AmericanExpress.com. If you have an American-Express-issued Card and have questions about this Online Privacy Statement, please call Customer Service at the phone number on the back of your Card. If you do not have a Card with American Express, you may call (800) 297–8378. This statement does not apply to those American Express sites that do not display or link to this statement or that have their own privacy statements.

Privacy Statement for American Express Card Holders

In addition to the protections that we provide through our Online Privacy Statement, your online activities may also be covered by one of our Privacy Notices, which is sent to you annually depending on which card(s) you may have. This Statement explains our collection, use, retention, and security of consumer information and applies to American Express products and services offered within the United States.

Exclusion of Financial Products or Services

The American Express Online Privacy Statement is not intended to be a legal notice for any American Express financial product or service. Certain financial products and services require a more specialized type of legal privacy notice, which provides specific details about particular personal financial products or services.

This Online Privacy Statement sets out our company policy regarding the collection and use of customer information on this website and applies to all services and pages available under the domain AmericanExpress.com.

To see the changes that we've made to this statement, go to Changes to Our Online Privacy Statement.

CUSTOMER PRIVACY PRINCIPLES

• **WE COLLECT ONLY CUSTOMER INFORMATION THAT IS NEEDED, AND WE TELL CUSTOMERS HOW WE USE IT.** We limit the collection of information about our customers to what we need to know to administer their accounts, to provide customer services, to offer new products and services, and to satisfy any legal and regulatory requirements. We also tell our customers about the general uses of information we collect about them, and we will provide additional explanation if customers request it.

• **WE GIVE CUSTOMERS CHOICES ABOUT HOW THEIR INFORMATION WILL BE USED.** Our businesses give customers "opt-out" choices about how information about the customer's relationship with that business unit may be used to generate marketing offers. These marketing choices include product and service offers from American Express businesses and those made by our business partners. Of course, each of our businesses will continue to send its customers information relating to products or services they receive from that business.

• **WE ENSURE INFORMATION QUALITY.** We use advanced technology, documented procedures and internal monitoring practices to help ensure that customer information is processed promptly, accurately and completely. We will respond in a timely manner to customers' requests to correct inaccurate account or transaction information. We also require high standards of quality from the consumer reporting agencies and others that provide us with information about prospective customers.

• **WE USE PRUDENT INFORMATION SECURITY SAFEGUARDS.** We limit access to customer information systems to those who specifically need it to conduct their business responsibilities, and to meet our customer servicing commitments. We employ safeguards designed to protect the confidentiality and security of our customer information.

• **WE LIMIT THE DISCLOSURE OF CUSTOMER INFORMATION.** We do not disclose customer information unless we have previously informed or been authorized by the customer, or we do so in connection with our efforts to reduce fraud or criminal activity and to comply with regulatory requirements and guidelines. When a court order or subpoena requires us to release information, we typically notify the customer to give the customer an opportunity to exercise his or her legal rights. Further, we will not disclose or use health information for marketing purposes or use it as a basis to make credit decisions.

• **WE ARE RESPONSIVE TO CUSTOMERS' REQUESTS FOR EXPLANATIONS.** If we deny an application for our services or end a customer's relationship with us, to the extent permitted by applicable law, we will provide an explanation, if requested. We state the reasons for the action taken and the information upon which the decision was based, unless the issue involves potential criminal activity.

• **WE HOLD OURSELVES RESPONSIBLE FOR OUR PRIVACY PRINCIPLES.** Each American Express employee is responsible for maintaining consumer confidence in the company. We provide training and communications programs designed to educate employees about the meaning and requirements of these Customer Privacy Principles. Employees who violate these Principles are subject to disciplinary action, up to and including dismissal. Employees are expected to report violations, and may do so confidentially, to their manager, to their business unit's compliance officer, or to the company's Office of the Ombudsperson.

We also conduct internal assessments of our privacy practices and periodically commission outside expert reviews of our compliance with the Privacy Principles and the specific policies and practices that support these Principles.

• **WE EXTEND THESE PRIVACY PRINCIPLES TO OUR BUSINESS RELATIONSHIPS.** We require companies we select as our business partners to agree to keep our customer information confidential and secure, to protect the information against unauthorized access, use, or re-disclosure by the recipient company, and limit its use to the purposes for which it was provided to them.

We also encourage our business partners to respect their customers' information by adopting strong and effective privacy policies and practices, including offering "opt-out" choices for marketing offers to their customers.

In addition, we participate actively in industry associations to advocate development of comprehensive privacy policies and implementation strategies.

SOURCE: American Express Company.

APPENDIX 11:
CODE OF ONLINE BUSINESS
PRACTICES—SELECTED PROVISIONS

PRINCIPLES FOR ETHICAL BUSINESS TO CUSTOMER CONDUCT

Principle I: Truthful and Accurate Communications

Online advertisers should not engage in deceptive or misleading trade practices with regard to any aspect of electronic commerce, including advertising, marketing, or in their use of technology.

A. Online advertisers should adhere to the Code of Advertising. Online advertisers should engage in truthful advertising. They should not make deceptive or misleading representations or omissions of material facts.

1. Online advertisers should be able to substantiate any express or reasonably implied factual claims made in their advertising or marketing and should possess reasonable substantiation prior to disseminating a claim.

2. Online advertisers should disclose their advertising or marketing to be such if failure to do so would be misleading.

3. If online advertisers make price comparisons, they should disclose the basis for, or the geographic area that constitutes, the market area. In all cases, online advertisers should either disclose the date when the comparison was made or if they offer ongoing claims, keep the substantiation current.

4. Online advertisers should cooperate with any bona fide, industry self-regulatory advertising programs where such programs exist to resolve any advertising disputes.

B. Online advertisers should use Internet technology to promote the customer's knowledge of the products or services being offered and should not use technology to mislead customers.

1. Online advertisers should not mislead online customers by creating the false impression of sponsorship, endorsement, popularity, trustworthiness, product quality or business size through the misuse of hyperlinks, "seals," other technology, or another's intellectual property.

2. Online advertisers may use hyperlinks to add to or supplement information about goods or services but should not misleadingly use hyperlinks or information provided via a hyperlink to: (a) contradict or substantially change the meaning of any material statement or claim; (b) create the false impression of affiliation; (c) create the false impression that the content, merchandise or service of another's business is their own.

3. Online advertisers should only use search terms or mechanisms that fairly reflect the content of their site.

4. Online advertisers should make sure that any third-party "seals" or endorsements that incorporate links to self-regulatory or ethical standard programs are functional so that customers can easily verify membership in the seal program and determine its purpose, scope, and standards. Any online advertiser that participates in any third-party self-regulatory or ethical standard or seal program should do so in conformity with that program's instructions regarding the display, activation, and uses of the seal or endorsement. If an express or implied claim is made through the use of a seal or text, the online advertiser should provide customers with the opportunity to understand the details behind the program, including the program's claims, scope and standards.

5. Online advertisers should not knowingly link to, or accept affinity or royalty payments from, deceptive, fraudulent, or illegal sites.

6. Online advertisers should not deceptively interfere with a customer's browser, computer, or any appliance the customer uses to access the Internet.

Principle II: Disclosure

Online merchants should disclose to their customers and prospective customers information about the business, the goods or services available for purchase online, and the transaction itself.

A. All information required by this Code should meet the following standards:

1. It should be clear, accurate, and easy to find and understand;

2. It should be readily accessible online and can appear via a noticeable and descriptive hyperlink or other similarly effective mechanism;

3. It should be presented such that customers can access and maintain an adequate record of it;

4. And, if the information relates to the goods or services available for purchase online or the transaction itself, it should be accessible prior to the consummation of the transaction.

B. Information About the Business:

1. Online merchants should provide, at a minimum, the following contact information online:

(a) legal name;

(b) the name under which it conducts business;

(c) the principle physical address or information, including country, sufficient to ensure the customer can locate the business offline;

(d) an online method of contact such as e-mail;

(e) a point of contact within the organization that is responsible for customer inquires; and

(f) a telephone number unless to do so would be disruptive to the operation of the business given its size and resources and then, the merchant should maintain a working listed phone number.

2. Online merchants that register an Internet domain name should provide complete and accurate information to the authorized Internet registrar with which they register and should use the appropriate top-level domain for the type of business registered.

C. Information About Goods and Services Available for Purchase Online:

Online merchants should provide enough information available about the goods or services available online so that customers can make an informed choice about whether to purchase such goods or services.

D. Information About the Online Transaction Itself:

Online merchants should provide enough information about the online transaction itself so that customers can make an informed choice about whether to engage in the online transaction.

1. Online merchants should disclose material information about the online transaction itself including, but not limited to:

(a) terms of the transaction;

(b) product availability/shipping information; and

(c) prices and customer costs.

2. Online merchants should provide the customer with an opportunity to:

(a) review and approve the transaction; and

(b) receive a confirmation.

3. If the online merchant chooses to provide some information in more than one language, all material information about the transaction should be available in the selected languages. Similarly, if the online merchant chooses to reach a particular population, such as the aged or handicapped, by using large font sizes or specific colors for example, all material information about the transaction should be provided in the same way.

E. Terms of the Online Transaction:

Online merchants should provide the terms of the online transaction including but not limited to:

1. Any restrictions or limitations they impose on the sale of the goods or services;

2. Easy-to-use payment mechanisms;

3. Return or refund policies, including how customers can make returns or exchanges; obtain refunds or credits; or cancel a transaction; and any associated time limitations or associated fees;.

4. For products, any warrantees, guarantees, escrow programs or other offered terms, including limitations, conditions, if any;

5. For services, any material standards, schedules, fees, or other offered terms, including limitation and conditions;

6. For contests, sweepstakes or other similar promotions, the complete rules adjacent to, or in a hyperlink or similar technology adjacent to, the promotion itself; and

7. For ongoing transactions or subscriptions:

(a) information about how the transaction will appear on the bill so that the customer can easily identify the business and the transaction on the bill; and

(b) easy-to-understand cancellation information, an easy to use means to cancel an ongoing subscription, and timely confirmation of such cancellation.

F. Product Availability/Terms of Shipping:

Online merchants should:

1. Note which products or services are temporarily unavailable and in those instances:

(a) provide information about when the customer will be charged for the transaction; and

(b) if an expected availability date is provided for unavailable products or services, have a reasonable basis for such date.

2. Have a reasonable basis for, and provide customers with, estimated shipping times (or in the case of online delivery, delivery times) (if such times are unknown at the time of the online transaction, the online merchant should provide the information via a timely follow-up e-mail but should provide the customer with the opportunity to cancel the transaction if the time indicated is unacceptable).

3. Have a reasonable basis for stated delivery claims when made.

4. Disclose any shipping, performance, or delivery limitations they impose (age, geographic).

5. If a material delay in shipping or performance occurs, provide the customer with timely information about the delay and the opportunity to cancel the transaction.

G. Prices and Customer Costs:

Online merchants should:

1. Disclose, in a specified currency, an itemized list of the prices or fees and expected customer costs to be collected by the online merchant with regard to an online transaction, including but not limited to:

(a) price or license fee to be charged, or in the case of a barter trade, the items that will be exchanged for goods or services purchased or licensed;

(b) expected shipping and handling charges (if such charges are unknown at the time of the online transaction, the online merchant should provide the information via a timely follow-up e-mail but should provide the customer with the opportunity to cancel the transaction if the costs are unacceptable); and

(c) expected taxes or other government imposed fees collected by the online merchant related to the transaction, etc.;

2. Provide a generalized description of other routine costs and fees related to the transaction that may be incurred by the customer such as tariffs or routine subscription fees that may not be collected by the online merchant;

3. Clearly identify the merchant's name and website address on any subsequent statements or other billing information; and

4. Honor the amount authorized by the customer in any subsequent bills to the customer.

H. Provide Opportunity to Review and Approve Transaction:

Prior to completion of the transaction, online merchants should provide customers with the option to review the online transaction and to confirm their intent to enter into the transaction by providing a summary that includes:

1. Information about the online transaction;

2. The selected payment method; and

3. The option to cancel or affirmatively complete the transaction.

I. Provide Confirmation of the Sale:

Online merchants should provide customers with the option to receive a confirmation of the transaction after the transaction has been completed. The confirmation should include:

1. A line-itemed statement of what was ordered, the price, and any other known charges such as shipping/handling and taxes,

2. Sufficient contact information to enable purchasers to obtain order status updates, and

3. The anticipated date of shipment.

Principle III: Information Practices and Security

Online advertisers should adopt information practices that treat customers' personal information with care. They should post and adhere to a privacy policy based on fair information principles, take appropriate measures to provide adequate security, and respect customers' preferences regarding unsolicited email.

A. Post and Adhere to a Privacy Policy:

Online advertisers should post and adhere to a privacy policy that is open, transparent, and meets generally accepted fair information principles including providing notice as to what personal information the online advertiser collects, uses, and discloses; what choices customers have with regard to the business' collection, use and, disclosure of that information; what access customers have to the information; what security measures are taken to protect the information, and what enforcement and redress mechanisms are in place to remedy any violations of the policy. The privacy policy should be easy to find and understand and be available prior to or at the time the customer provides any personally identifiable information.

B. Provide Adequate Security:

Online advertisers should use appropriate levels of security for the type of information collected, maintained, or transferred to third parties and should:

1. Use industry standard levels of encryption and authentication for the transfer or receipt of health care information, social security numbers, financial transaction information (for example, a credit card number), or other sensitive information,

2. Provide industry standard levels of security and integrity to protect data being maintained by computers, and

3. Take reasonable steps to require third parties involved in fulfilling a customer transaction to also maintain appropriate levels of security.

C. Respect Customer's Preferences Regarding Unsolicited E-mail:

Online advertisers should accurately describe their business practices with regard to their use of unsolicited e-mail to customers.

1. Online advertisers that engage in unsolicited email marketing should post and adhere to a "Do Not Contact" policy—a policy that, at a minimum, enables those customers who do not wish to be contacted online to "opt out" online from future solicitations. This policy should be available both on the website and in any emails, other than those relating to a particular order.

2. Online advertisers that engage in unsolicited email marketing should also subscribe to a bona-fide e-mail suppression list such as the one offered by the Direct Marketing Association (www.the-dma.org/). Additional resources on opt-outs generally, less on email, are offered by the Center for Democracy and Technology (http://opt-out.cdt.org/).

Principle IV: Customer Satisfaction

Online merchants should seek to ensure their customers are satisfied by honoring their representations, answering questions, and

resolving customer complaints and disputes in a timely and responsive manner.

A. Honor Representations: Online merchants should comply with all commitments, representations, and other promises made to a customer.

B. Answer Questions: Online merchants should provide an easy-to-find and understand notice of how customers can successfully and meaningfully contact the business to get answers to their questions. Online merchants should promptly and substantively respond to the customer's commercially reasonable questions.

C. Resolve Customer Complaints and Disputes: Online merchants should seek to resolve customer complaints and disputes in a fair, timely, and effective manner:

1. Online merchants should provide an easy-to-find and understandable notice of how a customer can successfully and meaningfully contact the business to expeditiously resolve complaints and disputes related to a transaction.

2. Online merchants shall have an effective and easy to use internal mechanism for addressing complaints and correcting errors.

3. In the event the customer's complaint cannot be resolved, online merchants shall also offer a fair method for resolving differences with regard to a transaction by offering either an unconditional money-back guarantee or third-party dispute resolution.

4. If an online merchant offers third party dispute resolution, it should use a trusted third party that offers impartial, accessible, and timely arbitration that is free to consumers or at a charge to consumers that is not disproportionate to the value of goods or services involved in the dispute.

5. Online merchants should provide customers with easy-to-find and understandable contact information for such third parties, including a link (or similar technology) to any third party sites used for such means.

Principle V: Protecting Children

If online advertisers target children under the age of 13, they should take special care to protect children by recognizing their developing cognitive abilities.

A. Online advertisers should adhere to the Children's Advertising Review Unit's ("CARU") Self Regulatory Guidelines for Children's Advertising.

B. Specifically, online advertisers should adhere to the Guidelines for Interactive Electronic Media that apply to online activities, which are intentionally targeted to children under 13, or where the website knows the visitor is a child. These Guidelines include parental permission first requirements in the "Making a Sale" and "Data Collection" provisions.

SOURCE: Council of Better Business Bureaus.

APPENDIX 12:
DIRECTORY OF ICPEN MEMBER COUNTRIES

COUNTRY	ADDRESS	TELEPHONE/FAX	E-MAIL	WEBSITE
AUSTRALIA	Australian Competition and Consumer Commission (ACCC) P.O. Box 1199k Dickson ACT 2602, Australia	+61 2 6243 1111 +61 2 6243 1196	Gst.complaints@accc.gov.au	None Listed
AUSTRIA	No Contact Information Listed			
AZERBAIJAN	No Contact Information Listed			www.antimonpoly.az
BELGIUM	Administration for Economic Inspection WTC III Boulevard Simon Bolivar 30 B-1000, Brussels, Belgium	+32-2-208.36.11 +32+2+208.39.15	eco.inspec@mineco.fgov.be	www.mineco.fgov. be/protection_consumer/ index_en.htm
CANADA	Canadian Competition Bureau 50 Victoria Street Gatineau, Quebec K1A 0C9, Canada	1-819-997-4282 1-819-997-0324	compbureau@ic.gc.ca	http://consumerinformation.ca

COUNTRY	ADDRESS	TELEPHONE/FAX	E-MAIL	WEBSITE
CHILE	Chile Consumer Protection Service Teatinos 50 Santiago, Chile	562-3519654 None Listed	sguerra@semac.cl	www.sernac.cl
CZECH REPUBLIC	No Contact Information Listed			
DENMARK	National Consumer Agency of Denmark Forbrugerstyreisen Amagerfaelledvej 56 2300 Copenhagen S Denmark	+45 32 66 90 00 +45 32 66 91 00	consumer@consumer.dk	www.consumer.dk
ESTONIA	Estonia Consumer Protection Board None Listed	372 620 1707 372 620 1701	info@consumer.ee	www.consumer.ee
FINLAND	Consumer Agency Haapaniemenkatu 4 A Bo 5, 00531 Helsinki, Finland	+358 9 7726 7821 +358 9 7726 7557	posti@kuluttajavirasto.fi	www.kuluttajavirasto.fi/ englanti
FRANCE	General Directorate for Competition Policy, Consumer Affairs and Fraud Control Ministry of the Economy, Finance and Industry 59 Boulevard Vincent Auriol Teledoc 031 F-75 703 Paris Cedex 13	+33 1 44 97 23 33 +33 1 44 97 34 67	concentrations@ dgccrf.finances.gouv.fr	www.dgccrf.bercy.gouv.fr

COUNTRY	ADDRESS	TELEPHONE/FAX	E-MAIL	WEBSITE
GERMANY	No Contact Information Listed			
GREECE	No Contact Information Listed			
HUNGARY	General Inspectorate for Consumer Protection 1088 Budapest, Jozsef krt. 6 Hungary	None Listed None Listed	fvf@fvf.hu	www.fvf.hu
IRELAND	National Consumer Agency 4 Harcourt Road Dublin 2, Ireland	+353 1 475 1444 +353 1 402 5501	ask@consumerconnect.ie	www.consumerconnect.ie
ITALY	No Contact Information Listed			
JAPAN	National Consumer Affairs Center of Japan None Listed	+81-3-3443-8623 +81-3-3443-8624	webmaster@kokusen.go.jp	www.kokusen.go.jp
LATVIA	Latvia Consumer Rights Protection Centre None Listed	+371 67212688 +371 67388634	ptac@ptac.gov.lv	www.ptac.gov.lv
LITHUANIA	National Consumer Rights Protection Board None Listed	+3702626751 +3702791466	taryba@nvtat.lt	www.nvtat.lt
LUXEMBOURG	No Contact Information Listed			

COUNTRY	ADDRESS	TELEPHONE/FAX	E-MAIL	WEBSITE
MALTA	Consumer and Competition Division Office for Fair Trading Cannon Road Santa Venera CMR 02, Malta	(+356) 21 446250-5 (+356) 21 482564	Barbara.r.buttigieg@gov.mt	None Listed
MEXICO	Procuraduria Federal de Consumidor Av. Jose Vasconcelos 208 Col Condesa Del. Cuauhtemoc, Mexico D.F. 06140	(52 5) 5 68 87 22 (52 5) 2 11 15 37	quejas@profeco.gov.mx	www.profeco.gov.mx
NETHERLANDS	Consumentenautoriteit Wijnhaven 24 Postbus 16759 2500 BT Den Haag	+31 70 330 5979 +31 70 330 5989	pers@consumentenautoriteit.nl	www.consumentenautoriteit.nl
NEW ZEALAND	Ministry of Consumer Affairs P.O. Box 1473 Wellington, New Zealand	64 4 924 3600 64 4 924 3700	mcainfo@mca.govt.nz	www.consumer-ministry.govt.nz
NORWAY	The Consumer Ombudsman and Market Council P.O. Box 4597 Nydalen, 0404 Oslo, Norway	+47 23 400 600 +47 23 400 601	fo@forbrukerombudet.dep.no	www.forbrukerombudet.no

COUNTRY	ADDRESS	TELEPHONE/FAX	E-MAIL	WEBSITE
POLAND	Office for Competition and Consumer Protection (OCCP) UOKiK/OCCP Pl. Powstańców Warszawy 1 00-950 Warszawa Poland	+48 022 55-60-800 +48 022 826-50-76	e_konsument@uokik.gov.pl	www.uokik.gov.pl
PORTUGAL	No Contact Information Listed			
SLOVAKIA	No Contact Information Listed			
SOUTH KOREA	Ministry of Finance and Economy (MOFE) 300-4 YeumGok-dong SeoCho-gu Seoul, Korea 137-700	82-2-3460-3413 82-2-3460-3419	econsumer@cpb.or.kr	http://kca.go.kr/jsp/eng/main.jsp
SPAIN	Ministerio de Sanidad y Consumo Centro de Publicaciones Paseo del Prado 18-20, 28014 Madrid, Spain	901 400 100 91 596 11 41	inc@consumoinc.es	www.msc.es/
SWEDEN	The Swedish Consumer Agency Box 48, SE-651 02 Karlstad, Sweden	+46 (0)771-42 33 00 +46 (0)54-19 41 95	konsumentverket@ konsumentverket.se	www.english. konsumentverket.se
SWITZERLAND	State Secretariat for Economic Affairs, Legal Affairs, and Trade Practices Effingerstrasse 1 CH—3003 Berne Switzerland	+41 (0)31 322 77 70 +41 (0)31 324 09 56	seco@seco.admin.ch	www.konsum.admin.ch/

COUNTRY	ADDRESS	TELEPHONE/FAX	E-MAIL	WEBSITE
UNITED KINGDOM	Office of Fair Trading Fleetbank House 2-6 Salisbury Square London EC4Y 8JX United Kingdom	08454 04 05 06 None Listed	enquiries@oft.gov.uk	www.oft.gov.uk
UNITED STATES	Federal Trade Commission Consumer Response Center 600 Pennsylvania Avenue, NW Washington, D.C. 20580	1-877-382-4357 1-202-326-2222	cpo@ftc.gov	www.ftc.gov

APPENDIX 13:
THE GRAMM-LEACH BLILEY ACT—
SELECTED PROVISIONS [15 U.S.C. § 6801]

15 U.S.C. § 6801. Protection of nonpublic personal information

(a) Privacy obligation policy

It is the policy of the Congress that each financial institution has an affirmative and continuing obligation to respect the privacy of its customers and to protect the security and confidentiality of those customers' nonpublic personal information.

(b) Financial institutions safeguards

In furtherance of the policy in subsection (a) of this section, each agency or authority described in section 6805(a) of this title shall establish appropriate standards for the financial institutions subject to their jurisdiction relating to administrative, technical, and physical safeguards—

> (1) to insure the security and confidentiality of customer records and information;

> (2) to protect against any anticipated threats or hazards to the security or integrity of such records; and

> (3) to protect against unauthorized access to or use of such records or information which could result in substantial harm or inconvenience to any customer.

15 U.S.C. § 6802. Obligations with respect to disclosures of personal information

(a) Notice requirements

Except as otherwise provided in this subchapter, a financial institution may not, directly or through any affiliate, disclose to a nonaffiliated third party any nonpublic personal information, unless such financial institution provides or has provided to the consumer a notice that complies with section 6803 of this title.

(b) Opt out

(1) In general

A financial institution may not disclose nonpublic personal information to a nonaffiliated third party unless—

(A) such financial institution clearly and conspicuously discloses to the consumer, in writing or in electronic form or other form permitted by the regulations prescribed under section 6804 of this title, that such information may be disclosed to such third party;

(B) the consumer is given the opportunity, before the time that such information is initially disclosed, to direct that such information not be disclosed to such third party; and

(C) the consumer is given an explanation of how the consumer can exercise that nondisclosure option.

(2) Exception

This subsection shall not prevent a financial institution from providing nonpublic personal information to a nonaffiliated third party to perform services for or functions on behalf of the financial institution, including marketing of the financial institution's own products or services, or financial products or services offered pursuant to joint agreements between two or more financial institutions that comply with the requirements imposed by the regulations prescribed under section 6804 of this title, if the financial institution fully discloses the providing of such information and enters into a contractual agreement with the third party that requires the third party to maintain the confidentiality of such information.

(c) Limits on reuse of information

Except as otherwise provided in this subchapter, a nonaffiliated third party that receives from a financial institution nonpublic personal information under this section shall not, directly or through an affiliate of such receiving third party, disclose such information to any other person that is a nonaffiliated third party of both the financial institution and such receiving third party, unless such disclosure would be lawful if made directly to such other person by the financial institution.

(d) Limitations on the sharing of account number information for marketing purposes

A financial institution shall not disclose, other than to a consumer reporting agency, an account number or similar form of access number or access code for a credit card account, deposit account, or transaction account of a consumer to any nonaffiliated third party for use in telemarketing, direct mail marketing, or other marketing through electronic mail to the consumer.

(e) General exceptions

Subsections (a) and (b) of this section shall not prohibit the disclosure of nonpublic personal information—

(1) as necessary to effect, administer, or enforce a transaction requested or authorized by the consumer, or in connection with—

(A) servicing or processing a financial product or service requested or authorized by the consumer;

(B) maintaining or servicing the consumer's account with the financial institution, or with another entity as part of a private label credit card program or other extension of credit on behalf of such entity; or

(C) a proposed or actual securitization, secondary market sale (including sales of servicing rights), or similar transaction related to a transaction of the consumer;

(2) with the consent or at the direction of the consumer;

(3)(A) to protect the confidentiality or security of the financial institution's records pertaining to the consumer, the service or product, or the transaction therein; (B) to protect against or prevent actual or potential fraud, unauthorized transactions, claims, or other liability; (C) for required institutional risk control, or for resolving customer disputes or inquiries; (D) to persons holding a legal or beneficial interest relating to the consumer; or (E) to persons acting in a fiduciary or representative capacity on behalf of the consumer;

(4) to provide information to insurance rate advisory organizations, guaranty funds or agencies, applicable rating agencies of the financial institution, persons assessing the institution's compliance with industry standards, and the institution's attorneys, accountants, and auditors;

(5) to the extent specifically permitted or required under other provisions of law and in accordance with the Right to Financial Privacy

Act of 1978 (12 U.S.C. § 3401 et seq.), to law enforcement agencies (including a Federal functional regulator, the Secretary of the Treasury with respect to subchapter II of chapter 53 of title 31, and chapter 2 of title I of Public Law 91-508 (12 U.S.C. § 1951–1959), a State insurance authority, or the Federal Trade Commission), self-regulatory organizations, or for an investigation on a matter related to public safety;

(6)(A) to a consumer reporting agency in accordance with the Fair Credit Reporting Act (15 U.S.C. § 1681 et seq.), or (B) from a consumer report reported by a consumer reporting agency;

(7) in connection with a proposed or actual sale, merger, transfer, or exchange of all or a portion of a business or operating unit if the disclosure of nonpublic personal information concerns solely consumers of such business or unit; or

(8) to comply with Federal, State, or local laws, rules, and other applicable legal requirements; to comply with a properly authorized civil, criminal, or regulatory investigation or subpoena or summons by Federal, State, or local authorities; or to respond to judicial process or government regulatory authorities having jurisdiction over the financial institution for examination, compliance, or other purposes as authorized by law.

15 U.S.C. § 6803. Disclosure of institution privacy policy

(a) Disclosure required

At the time of establishing a customer relationship with a consumer and not less than annually during the continuation of such relationship, a financial institution shall provide a clear and conspicuous disclosure to such consumer, in writing or in electronic form or other form permitted by the regulations prescribed under section 6804 of this title, of such financial institution's policies and practices with respect to—

(1) disclosing nonpublic personal information to affiliates and non-affiliated third parties, consistent with section 6802 of this title, including the categories of information that may be disclosed;

(2) disclosing nonpublic personal information of persons who have ceased to be customers of the financial institution; and

(3) protecting the nonpublic personal information of consumers.

(b) Regulations

Disclosures required by subsection (a) of this section shall be made in accordance with the regulations prescribed under section 6804 of this title.

(c) Information to be included

The disclosure required by subsection (a) shall include—

(1) the policies and practices of the institution with respect to disclosing nonpublic personal information to nonaffiliated third parties, other than agents of the institution, consistent with section 6802 of this title, and including—

(A) the categories of persons to whom the information is or may be disclosed, other than the persons to whom the information may be provided pursuant to section 6802(e) of this title; and

(B) the policies and practices of the institution with respect to disclosing of nonpublic personal information of persons who have ceased to be customers of the financial institution;

(2) the categories of nonpublic personal information that are collected by the financial institution;

(3) the policies that the institution maintains to protect the confidentiality and security of nonpublic personal information in accordance with section 6801 of this title; and

(4) the disclosures required, if any, under section 1681a(d)(2)(A)(iii) of this title.

(d) Exemption for certified public accountants

(1) In general

The disclosure requirements of subsection (a) do not apply to any person, to the extent that the person is—

(A) a certified public accountant;

(B) certified or licensed for such purpose by a State; and

(C) subject to any provision of law, rule, or regulation issued by a legislative or regulatory body of the State, including rules of professional conduct or ethics, that prohibits disclosure of nonpublic personal information without the knowing and expressed consent of the consumer.

(2) Limitation

Nothing in this subsection shall be construed to exempt or otherwise exclude any financial institution that is affiliated or becomes affiliated with a certified public accountant described in paragraph (1) from any provision of this section.

(3) Definitions

For purposes of this subsection, the term "State" means any State or territory of the United States, the District of Columbia, Puerto Rico, Guam, American Samoa, the Trust Territory of the Pacific Islands, the Virgin Islands, or the Northern Mariana Islands.

(e) Model forms

(1) In general

The agencies referred to in section 6804(a)(1) of this title shall jointly develop a model form which may be used, at the option of the financial institution, for the provision of disclosures under this section.

(2) Format

A model form developed under paragraph (1) shall—

(A) be comprehensible to consumers, with a clear format and design;

(B) provide for clear and conspicuous disclosures;

(C) enable consumers easily to identify the sharing practices of a financial institution and to compare privacy practices among financial institutions; and

(D) be succinct, and use an easily readable type font.

(3) Timing

A model form required to be developed by this subsection shall be issued in proposed form for public comment not later than 180 days after October 13, 2006.

(4) Safe harbor

Any financial institution that elects to provide the model form developed by the agencies under this subsection shall be deemed to be in compliance with the disclosures required under this section.

15 U.S.C. § 6804. Rulemaking

(a) Regulatory authority

(1) Rulemaking

The Federal banking agencies, the National Credit Union Administration, the Secretary of the Treasury, the Securities and Exchange Commission, and the Federal Trade Commission shall each prescribe, after consultation as appropriate with representatives of State insurance authorities designated by the National Association of Insurance Commissioners, such regulations as may be necessary to carry out the purposes of this subchapter with respect to the financial institutions subject to their jurisdiction under section 6805 of this title.

(2) Coordination, consistency, and comparability

Each of the agencies and authorities required under paragraph (1) to prescribe regulations shall consult and coordinate with the other such agencies and authorities for the purposes of assuring, to the extent possible, that the regulations prescribed by each such agency and authority are consistent and comparable with the regulations prescribed by the other such agencies and authorities.

(3) Procedures and deadline

Such regulations shall be prescribed in accordance with applicable requirements of title 5 and shall be issued in final form not later than 6 months after November 12, 1999.

(b) Authority to grant exceptions

The regulations prescribed under subsection (a) of this section may include such additional exceptions to subsections (a) through (d) of section 6802 of this title as are deemed consistent with the purposes of this subchapter.

15 U.S.C. § 6805. Enforcement

(a) In general

This subchapter and the regulations prescribed thereunder shall be enforced by the Federal functional regulators, the State insurance authorities, and the Federal Trade Commission with respect to financial institutions and other persons subject to their jurisdiction under applicable law, as follows:

(1) Under section 1818 of title 12, in the case of—

(A) national banks, Federal branches and Federal agencies of foreign banks, and any subsidiaries of such entities (except brokers, dealers, persons providing insurance, investment companies, and investment advisers), by the Office of the Comptroller of the Currency;

(B) member banks of the Federal Reserve System (other than national banks), branches and agencies of foreign banks (other than Federal branches, Federal agencies, and insured State branches of foreign banks), commercial lending companies owned or controlled by foreign banks, organizations operating under section 25 or 25A of the Federal Reserve Act (12 U.S.C. § 601 et seq., 611 et seq.), and bank holding companies and their nonbank subsidiaries or affiliates (except brokers, dealers, persons providing insurance, investment companies, and investment advisers), by the Board of Governors of the Federal Reserve System;

(C) banks insured by the Federal Deposit Insurance Corporation (other than members of the Federal Reserve System), insured State branches of foreign banks, and any subsidiaries of such entities (except brokers, dealers, persons providing insurance, investment companies, and investment advisers), by the Board of Directors of the Federal Deposit Insurance Corporation; and

(D) savings associations the deposits of which are insured by the Federal Deposit Insurance Corporation, and any subsidiaries of such savings associations (except brokers, dealers, persons providing insurance, investment companies, and investment advisers), by the Director of the Office of Thrift Supervision.

(2) Under the Federal Credit Union Act (12 U.S.C. § 1751 et seq.), by the Board of the National Credit Union Administration with respect to any federally insured credit union, and any subsidiaries of such an entity.

(3) Under the Securities Exchange Act of 1934 (15 U.S.C. § 78a et seq.), by the Securities and Exchange Commission with respect to any broker or dealer.

(4) Under the Investment Company Act of 1940 (15 U.S.C. § 80a-1 et seq.), by the Securities and Exchange Commission with respect to investment companies.

(5) Under the Investment Advisers Act of 1940 (15 U.S.C. § 80b-1 et seq.), by the Securities and Exchange Commission with respect to investment advisers registered with the Commission under such Act.

(6) Under State insurance law, in the case of any person engaged in providing insurance, by the applicable State insurance authority of the State in which the person is domiciled, subject to section 6701 of this title.

(7) Under the Federal Trade Commission Act (15 U.S.C. § 41 et seq.), by the Federal Trade Commission for any other financial institution or other person that is not subject to the jurisdiction of any agency or authority under paragraphs (1) through (6) of this subsection.

(b) Enforcement of section 6801

(1) In general

Except as provided in paragraph (2), the agencies and authorities described in subsection (a) of this section shall implement the standards prescribed under section 6801(b) of this title in the same manner, to the extent practicable, as standards prescribed pursuant to section 1831p-1(a) of title 12 are implemented pursuant to such section.

(2) Exception

The agencies and authorities described in paragraphs (3), (4), (5), (6), and (7) of subsection (a) of this section shall implement the standards prescribed under section 6801(b) of this title by rule with respect to the financial institutions and other persons subject to their respective jurisdictions under subsection (a) of this section.

(c) Absence of State action

If a State insurance authority fails to adopt regulations to carry out this subchapter, such State shall not be eligible to override, pursuant to section 1831x(g)(2)(B)(iii) of title 12, the insurance customer protection regulations prescribed by a Federal banking agency under section 1831x(a) of title 12.

(d) Definitions

The terms used in subsection (a)(1) of this section that are not defined in this subchapter or otherwise defined in section 1813(s) of title 12 shall have the same meaning as given in section 3101 of title 12.

15 U.S.C. § 6806. Relation to other provisions

Except for the amendments made by subsections (a) and (b), nothing in this chapter shall be construed to modify, limit, or supersede the operation of the Fair Credit Reporting Act (15 U.S.C. § 1681 et seq.), and no inference shall be drawn on the basis of the provisions of this chapter regarding whether information is transaction or experience information under section 603 of such Act (15 U.S.C. § 1681a).

15 U.S.C. § 6807. Relation to State laws

(a) In general

This subchapter and the amendments made by this subchapter shall not be construed as superseding, altering, or affecting any statute, regulation, order, or interpretation in effect in any State, except to the extent that such statute, regulation, order, or interpretation is inconsistent with the provisions of this subchapter, and then only to the extent of the inconsistency.

(b) Greater protection under State law

For purposes of this section, a State statute, regulation, order, or interpretation is not inconsistent with the provisions of this subchapter if the protection such statute, regulation, order, or interpretation affords any person is greater than the protection provided under this subchapter and the amendments made by this subchapter, as determined by the Federal Trade Commission, after consultation with the agency or authority with jurisdiction under section 6805(a) of this title of either the person that initiated the complaint or that is the subject of the complaint, on its own motion or upon the petition of any interested party.

15 U.S.C. § 6808. Study of information sharing among financial affiliates

(a) In general

The Secretary of the Treasury, in conjunction with the Federal functional regulators and the Federal Trade Commission, shall conduct a study of information sharing practices among financial institutions and their affiliates. Such study shall include—

(1) the purposes for the sharing of confidential customer information with affiliates or with nonaffiliated third parties;

(2) the extent and adequacy of security protections for such information;

(3) the potential risks for customer privacy of such sharing of information;

(4) the potential benefits for financial institutions and affiliates of such sharing of information;

(5) the potential benefits for customers of such sharing of information;

(6) the adequacy of existing laws to protect customer privacy;

(7) the adequacy of financial institution privacy policy and privacy rights disclosure under existing law;

(8) the feasibility of different approaches, including opt-out and opt-in, to permit customers to direct that confidential information not be shared with affiliates and nonaffiliated third parties; and

(9) the feasibility of restricting sharing of information for specific uses or of permitting customers to direct the uses for which information may be shared.

(b) Consultation

The Secretary shall consult with representatives of State insurance authorities designated by the National Association of Insurance Commissioners, and also with financial services industry, consumer organizations and privacy groups, and other representatives of the general public, in formulating and conducting the study required by subsection (a) of this section.

(c) Report

On or before January 1, 2002, the Secretary shall submit a report to the Congress containing the findings and conclusions of the study required under subsection (a) of this section, together with such recommendations for legislative or administrative action as may be appropriate.

15 U.S.C. § 6809. Definitions

As used in this subchapter:

(1) Federal banking agency

The term "Federal banking agency" has the same meaning as given in section 1813 of title 12.

(2) Federal functional regulator

The term "Federal functional regulator" means—

(A) the Board of Governors of the Federal Reserve System;

(B) the Office of the Comptroller of the Currency;

(C) the Board of Directors of the Federal Deposit Insurance Corporation;

(D) the Director of the Office of Thrift Supervision;

(E) the National Credit Union Administration Board; and

(F) the Securities and Exchange Commission.

(3) Financial institution

(A) In general

The term "financial institution" means any institution the business of which is engaging in financial activities as described in section 1843(k) of title 12.

(B) Persons subject to CFTC regulation

Notwithstanding subparagraph (A), the term "financial institution" does not include any person or entity with respect to any financial activity that is subject to the jurisdiction of the Commodity Futures Trading Commission under the Commodity Exchange Act (7 U.S.C. § 1 et seq.).

(C) Farm credit institutions

Notwithstanding subparagraph (A), the term "financial institution" does not include the Federal Agricultural Mortgage Corporation or any entity chartered and operating under the Farm Credit Act of 1971 (12 U.S.C. § 2001 et seq.).

(D) Other secondary market institutions

Notwithstanding subparagraph (A), the term "financial institution" does not include institutions chartered by Congress specifically to engage in transactions described in section 6802(e)(1)(C) of this title, as long as such institutions do not sell or transfer nonpublic personal information to a nonaffiliated third party.

(4) Nonpublic personal information

(A) The term "nonpublic personal information" means personally identifiable financial information—

(i) provided by a consumer to a financial institution;

(ii) resulting from any transaction with the consumer or any service performed for the consumer; or

(iii) otherwise obtained by the financial institution.

(B) Such term does not include publicly available information, as such term is defined by the regulations prescribed under section 6804 of this title.

(C) Notwithstanding subparagraph (B), such term—

(i) shall include any list, description, or other grouping of consumers (and publicly available information pertaining to them) that is derived using any nonpublic personal information other than publicly available information; but

(ii) shall not include any list, description, or other grouping of consumers (and publicly available information pertaining to them) that is derived without using any nonpublic personal information.

(5) Nonaffiliated third party

The term "nonaffiliated third party" means any entity that is not an affiliate of, or related by common ownership or affiliated by corporate control with, the financial institution, but does not include a joint employee of such institution.

(6) Affiliate

The term "affiliate" means any company that controls, is controlled by, or is under common control with another company.

(7) Necessary to effect, administer, or enforce

The term "as necessary to effect, administer, or enforce the transaction" means—

(A) the disclosure is required, or is a usual, appropriate, or acceptable method, to carry out the transaction or the product or service business of which the transaction is a part, and record or service or maintain the consumer's account in the ordinary course of providing the financial service or financial product, or to administer or service benefits or claims relating to the transaction or the product or service business of which it is a part, and includes—

(i) providing the consumer or the consumer's agent or broker with a confirmation, statement, or other record of the transaction, or information on the status or value of the financial service or financial product; and

(ii) the accrual or recognition of incentives or bonuses associated with the transaction that are provided by the financial institution or any other party;

(B) the disclosure is required, or is one of the lawful or appropriate methods, to enforce the rights of the financial institution or of other persons engaged in carrying out the financial transaction, or providing the product or service;

(C) the disclosure is required, or is a usual, appropriate, or acceptable method, for insurance underwriting at the consumer's request or for reinsurance purposes, or for any of the following purposes as they relate to a consumer's insurance: Account administration, reporting, investigating, or preventing fraud or material misrepresentation, processing premium payments, processing insurance claims, administering insurance benefits (including utilization review activities), participating in research projects, or as otherwise required or specifically permitted by Federal or State law; or

(D) the disclosure is required, or is a usual, appropriate or acceptable method, in connection with—

(i) the authorization, settlement, billing, processing, clearing, transferring, reconciling, or collection of amounts charged, debited, or otherwise paid using a debit, credit or other payment card, check, or account number, or by other payment means;

(ii) the transfer of receivables, accounts or interests therein; or

(iii) the audit of debit, credit or other payment information.

(8) State insurance authority

The term "State insurance authority" means, in the case of any person engaged in providing insurance, the State insurance authority of the State in which the person is domiciled.

(9) Consumer

The term "consumer" means an individual who obtains, from a financial institution, financial products or services which are to be used primarily for personal, family, or household purposes, and also means the legal representative of such an individual.

(10) Joint agreement

The term "joint agreement" means a formal written contract pursuant to which two or more financial institutions jointly offer, endorse, or sponsor a financial product or service, and as may be further defined in the regulations prescribed under section 6804 of this title.

(11) Customer relationship

The term "time of establishing a customer relationship" shall be defined by the regulations prescribed under section 6804 of this title, and shall, in the case of a financial institution engaged in extending credit directly to consumers to finance purchases of goods or services, mean the time of establishing the credit relationship with the consumer.

***

15 U.S.C. § 6821. Privacy protection for customer information of financial institutions

(a) Prohibition on obtaining customer information by false pretenses

It shall be a violation of this subchapter for any person to obtain or attempt to obtain, or cause to be disclosed or attempt to cause to be disclosed to any person, customer information of a financial institution relating to another person—

(1) by making a false, fictitious, or fraudulent statement or representation to an officer, employee, or agent of a financial institution;

(2) by making a false, fictitious, or fraudulent statement or representation to a customer of a financial institution; or

(3) by providing any document to an officer, employee, or agent of a financial institution, knowing that the document is forged, counterfeit, lost, or stolen, was fraudulently obtained, or contains a false, fictitious, or fraudulent statement or representation.

(b) Prohibition on solicitation of a person to obtain customer information from financial institution under false pretenses

It shall be a violation of this subchapter to request a person to obtain customer information of a financial institution, knowing that the person will obtain, or attempt to obtain, the information from the institution in any manner described in subsection (a) of this section.

(c) Nonapplicability to law enforcement agencies

No provision of this section shall be construed so as to prevent any action by a law enforcement agency, or any officer, employee, or agent of such agency, to obtain customer information of a financial institution in connection with the performance of the official duties of the agency.

(d) Nonapplicability to financial institutions in certain cases

No provision of this section shall be construed so as to prevent any financial institution, or any officer, employee, or agent of a financial institution, from obtaining customer information of such financial institution in the course of—

(1) testing the security procedures or systems of such institution for maintaining the confidentiality of customer information;

(2) investigating allegations of misconduct or negligence on the part of any officer, employee, or agent of the financial institution; or

(3) recovering customer information of the financial institution which was obtained or received by another person in any manner described in subsection (a) or (b) of this section.

(e) Nonapplicability to insurance institutions for investigation of insurance fraud

No provision of this section shall be construed so as to prevent any insurance institution, or any officer, employee, or agency of an insurance institution, from obtaining information as part of an insurance investigation into criminal activity, fraud, material misrepresentation, or material nondisclosure that is authorized for such institution under State law, regulation, interpretation, or order.

(f) Nonapplicability to certain types of customer information of financial institutions

No provision of this section shall be construed so as to prevent any person from obtaining customer information of a financial institution that otherwise is available as a public record filed pursuant to the securities laws (as defined in section 78c(a)(47) of this title).

(g) Nonapplicability to collection of child support judgments

No provision of this section shall be construed to prevent any State-licensed private investigator, or any officer, employee, or agent of such private investigator, from obtaining customer information of a financial institution, to the extent reasonably necessary to collect child support from a person adjudged to have been delinquent in his or her obligations by a Federal or State court, and to the extent that such action by a State-licensed private investigator is not unlawful under any other Federal or State law or regulation, and has been authorized by an order or judgment of a court of competent jurisdiction.

15 U.S.C. § 6822. Administrative enforcement

(a) Enforcement by Federal Trade Commission

Except as provided in subsection (b) of this section, compliance with this subchapter shall be enforced by the Federal Trade Commission in the same manner and with the same power and authority as the Commission has under the Fair Debt Collection Practices Act [15 U.S.C. 1692 et seq.] to enforce compliance with such Act.

(b) Enforcement by other agencies in certain cases

(1) In general

Compliance with this subchapter shall be enforced under—

(A) Section 8 of the Federal Deposit Insurance Act [12 U.S.C. 1818], in the case of—

(i) National banks, and Federal branches and Federal agencies of foreign banks, by the Office of the Comptroller of the Currency;

(ii) Member banks of the Federal Reserve System (other than national banks), branches and agencies of foreign banks (other than Federal branches, Federal agencies, and insured State branches of foreign banks), commercial lending companies owned or controlled by foreign banks, and organizations operating under section 25 or 25A of the Federal Reserve Act [12 U.S.C. 601 et seq., 611 et seq.], by the Board;

(iii) banks insured by the Federal Deposit Insurance Corporation (other than members of the Federal Reserve System and national nonmember banks) and insured State branches of foreign banks, by the Board of Directors of the Federal Deposit Insurance Corporation; and

(iv) savings associations the deposits of which are insured by the Federal Deposit Insurance Corporation, by the Director of the Office of Thrift Supervision; and

(B) the Federal Credit Union Act [12 U.S.C. 1751 et seq.], by the Administrator of the National Credit Union Administration with respect to any Federal credit union.

(2) Violations of this subchapter treated as violations of other laws

For the purpose of the exercise by any agency referred to in paragraph (1) of its powers under any Act referred to in that paragraph, a violation of this subchapter shall be deemed to be a violation of a requirement imposed under that Act. In addition to its powers under any provision of law specifically referred to in paragraph (1), each of the agencies referred to in that paragraph may exercise, for the purpose of enforcing compliance with this subchapter, any other authority conferred on such agency by law.

15 U.S.C. § 6823. Criminal penalty

(a) In general

Whoever knowingly and intentionally violates, or knowingly and intentionally attempts to violate, section 6821 of this title shall be fined in accordance with title 18 or imprisoned for not more than 5 years, or both.

(b) Enhanced penalty for aggravated cases

Whoever violates, or attempts to violate, section 6821 of this title while violating another law of the United States or as part of a pattern of any illegal activity involving more than $100,000 in a 12-month period shall be fined twice the amount provided in subsection (b)(3) or (c)(3) (as the case may be) of section 3571 of title 18, imprisoned for not more than 10 years, or both.

15 U.S.C. § 6824. Relation to State laws

(a) In general

This subchapter shall not be construed as superseding, altering, or affecting the statutes, regulations, orders, or interpretations in effect in any State, except to the extent that such statutes, regulations, orders, or interpretations are inconsistent with the provisions of this subchapter, and then only to the extent of the inconsistency.

(b) Greater protection under State law

For purposes of this section, a State statute, regulation, order, or interpretation is not inconsistent with the provisions of this subchapter if the protection such statute, regulation, order, or interpretation affords any person is greater than the protection provided under this subchapter as determined by the Federal Trade Commission, after consultation with the agency or authority with jurisdiction under section 6822 of this title of either the person that initiated the complaint or that is the subject of the complaint, on its own motion or upon the petition of any interested party.

15 U.S.C. § 6825. Agency guidance

In furtherance of the objectives of this subchapter, each Federal banking agency (as defined in section 1813(z) of title 12), the National Credit Union Administration, and the Securities and Exchange Commission or self-regulatory organizations, as appropriate, shall review regulations and guidelines applicable to financial institutions under their respective jurisdictions and shall prescribe such revisions to such regulations and guidelines as may be necessary to ensure that such financial institutions have policies, procedures, and controls in place to prevent the unauthorized disclosure of customer financial information and to deter and detect activities proscribed under section 6821 of this title.

15 U.S.C. § 6826. Reports

(a) Report to the Congress

Before the end of the 18-month period beginning on November 12, 1999, the Comptroller General, in consultation with the Federal Trade Commission, Federal banking agencies, the National Credit Union Administration, the Securities and Exchange Commission, appropriate Federal law enforcement agencies, and appropriate State insurance regulators, shall submit to the Congress a report on the following:

(1) The efficacy and adequacy of the remedies provided in this subchapter in addressing attempts to obtain financial information by fraudulent means or by false pretenses.

(2) Any recommendations for additional legislative or regulatory action to address threats to the privacy of financial information created by attempts to obtain information by fraudulent means or false pretenses.

(b) Annual report by administering agencies

The Federal Trade Commission and the Attorney General shall submit to Congress an annual report on number and disposition of all enforcement actions taken pursuant to this subchapter.

15 U.S.C. § 6827. Definitions

For purposes of this subchapter, the following definitions shall apply:

(1) Customer

The term "customer" means, with respect to a financial institution, any person (or authorized representative of a person) to whom the financial institution provides a product or service, including that of acting as a fiduciary.

(2) Customer information of a financial institution

The term "customer information of a financial institution" means any information maintained by or for a financial institution which is derived from the relationship between the financial institution and a customer of the financial institution and is identified with the customer.

(3) Document

The term "document" means any information in any form.

(4) Financial institution

(A) In general

The term "financial institution" means any institution engaged in the business of providing financial services to customers who maintain a credit, deposit, trust, or other financial account or relationship with the institution.

(B) Certain financial institutions specifically included

The term "financial institution" includes any depository institution (as defined in section 461(b)(1)(A) of title 12), any broker or dealer, any investment adviser or investment company, any insurance company, any loan or finance company, any credit card issuer or operator of a credit card system, and any consumer reporting agency that compiles and maintains files on consumers on a nationwide basis (as defined in section 1681a(p) of this title).

(C) Securities institutions

For purposes of subparagraph (B)—

(i) the terms "broker" and "dealer" have the same meanings as given in section 78c of this title;

(ii) the term "investment adviser" has the same meaning as given in section 80b-2(a)(11) of this title; and

(iii) the term "investment company" has the same meaning as given in section 80a-3 of this title.

(D) Certain persons and entities specifically excluded

The term "financial institution" does not include any person or entity with respect to any financial activity that is subject to the jurisdiction of the Commodity Futures Trading Commission under the Commodity Exchange Act (7 U.S.C. § 1 et seq.) and does not include the Federal Agricultural Mortgage Corporation or any entity chartered and operating under the Farm Credit Act of 1971 (12 U.S.C. § 2001 et seq.).

(E) Further definition by regulation

The Federal Trade Commission, after consultation with Federal banking agencies and the Securities and Exchange Commission, may prescribe regulations clarifying or describing the types of institutions which shall be treated as financial institutions for purposes of this subchapter.

APPENDIX 14:
THE CHILDREN'S ONLINE PRIVACY PROTECTION ACT (COPPA)
[15 U.S.C. § 6501–6506]

SEC. 1301. SHORT TITLE.

This title may be cited as the "Children's Online Privacy Protection Act of 1998."

SEC. 1302. DEFINITIONS.

In this title:

(1) CHILD.—The term "child" means an individual under the age of 13.

(2) OPERATOR.—The term "operator"—

(A) means any person who operates a website located on the Internet or an online service and who collects or maintains personal information from or about the users of or visitors to such website or online service, or on whose behalf such information is collected or maintained, where such website or online service is operated for commercial purposes, including any person offering products or services for sale through that website or online service, involving commerce—

(i) among the several States or with 1 or more foreign nations;

(ii) in any territory of the United States or in the District of Columbia, or between any such territory and—

(I) another such territory; or

(II) any State or foreign nation; or

(iii) between the District of Columbia and any State, territory, or foreign nation; but

(B) does not include any nonprofit entity that would otherwise be exempt from coverage under section 5 of the Federal Trade Commission Act (15 U.S.C. 45).

(3) COMMISSION.—The term "Commission" means the Federal Trade Commission.

(4) DISCLOSURE.—The term "disclosure" means, with respect to personal information—

(A) the release of personal information collected from a child in identifiable form by an operator for any purpose, except where such information is provided to a person other than the operator who provides support for the internal operations of the website and does not disclose or use that information for any other purpose; and

(B) making personal information collected from a child by a website or online service directed to children or with actual knowledge that such information was collected from a child, publicly available in identifiable form, by any means including by a public posting, through the Internet, or through—

(i) a home page of a website;

(ii) a pen pal service;

(iii) an electronic mail service;

(iv) a message board; or

(v) a chat room.

(5) FEDERAL AGENCY.—The term "Federal agency" means an agency, as that term is defined in section 551(1) of title 5, United States Code.

(6) INTERNET.—The term "Internet" means collectively the myriad of computer and telecommunications facilities, including equipment and operating software, which comprise the interconnected worldwide network of networks that employ the Transmission Control Protocol/ Internet Protocol, or any predecessor or successor protocols to such protocol, to communicate information of all kinds by wire or radio.

(7) PARENT.—The term "parent" includes a legal guardian.

(8) PERSONAL INFORMATION.—The term "personal information" means individually identifiable information about an individual collected online, including—

(A) a first and last name;

(B) a home or other physical address including street name and name of a city or town;

(C) an e-mail address;

(D) a telephone number;

(E) a Social Security number;

(F) any other identifier that the Commission determines permits the physical or online contacting of a specific individual; or

(G) information concerning the child or the parents of that child that the website collects online from the child and combines with an identifier described in this paragraph.

(9) VERIFIABLE PARENTAL CONSENT.—The term "verifiable parental consent" means any reasonable effort (taking into consideration available technology), including a request for authorization for future collection, use, and disclosure described in the notice, to ensure that a parent of a child receives notice of the operator's personal information collection, use, and disclosure practices, and authorizes the collection, use, and disclosure, as applicable, of personal information and the subsequent use of that information before that information is collected from that child.

(10) WEBSITE OR ONLINE SERVICE DIRECTED TO CHILDREN.—

(A) IN GENERAL.—The term "website or online service directed to children" means—

(i) a commercial website or online service that is targeted to children; or

(ii) that portion of a commercial website or online service that is targeted to children.

(B) LIMITATION.—A commercial website or online service, or a portion of a commercial website or online service, shall not be deemed directed to children solely for referring or linking to a commercial website or online service directed to children by using information location tools, including a directory, index, reference, pointer, or hypertext link.

---

(11) PERSON.—The term "person" means any individual, partnership, corporation, trust, estate, cooperative, association, or other entity.

(12) ONLINE CONTACT INFORMATION.—The term "online contact information" means an e-mail address or an-other substantially similar identifier that permits direct contact with a person online.

SEC. 1303. REGULATION OF UNFAIR AND DECEPTIVE ACTS AND PRACTICES IN CONNECTION WITH THE COLLECTION AND USE OF PERSONAL INFORMATION FROM AND ABOUT CHILDREN ON THE INTERNET.

(a) ACTS PROHIBITED.—

(1) IN GENERAL.—It is unlawful for an operator of a website or online service directed to children, or any operator that has actual knowledge that it is collecting personal information from a child, to collect personal information from a child in a manner that violates the regulations prescribed under subsection (b).

(2) DISCLOSURE TO PARENT PROTECTED.—Notwithstanding paragraph (1), neither an operator of such a website or online service nor the operator's agent shall be held to be liable under any Federal or State law for any disclosure made in good faith and following reasonable procedures in responding to a request for disclosure of personal information under subsection (b)(1)(B)(iii) to the parent of a child.

(b) REGULATIONS.—

(1) IN GENERAL.—Not later than 1 year after the date of the enactment of this Act, the Commission shall promulgate under section 553 of title 5, United States Code, regulations that—

(A) require the operator of any website or online service directed to children that collects personal information from children or the operator of a website or online service that has actual knowledge that it is collecting personal information from a child—

(i) to provide notice on the website of what information is collected from children by the operator, how the operator uses such information, and the operator's disclosure practices for such information; and

(ii) to obtain verifiable parental consent for the collection, use, or disclosure of personal information from children;

(B) require the operator to provide, upon request of a parent under this subparagraph whose child has provided personal information to that website or online service, upon proper identification of that parent, to such parent—

(i) a description of the specific types of personal information collected from the child by that operator;

(ii) the opportunity at any time to refuse to permit the operator's further use or maintenance in retrievable form, or future online collection, of personal information from that child; and

(iii) notwithstanding any other provision of law, a means that is reasonable under the circumstances for the parent to obtain any personal information collected from that child;

(C) prohibit conditioning a child's participation in a game, the offering of a prize, or another activity on the child disclosing more personal information than is reasonably necessary to participate in such activity; and

(D) require the operator of such a website or online service to establish and maintain reasonable procedures to protect the confidentiality, security, and integrity of personal information collected from children.

(2) WHEN CONSENT NOT REQUIRED.—The regulations shall provide that verifiable parental consent under paragraph (1)(A)(ii) is not required in the case of—

(A) online contact information collected from a child that is used only to respond directly on a one-time basis to a specific request from the child and is not used to recontact the child and is not maintained in retrievable form by the operator;

(B) a request for the name or online contact information of a parent or child that is used for the sole purpose of obtaining parental consent or providing notice under this section and where such information is not maintained in retrievable form by the operator if parental consent is not obtained after a reasonable time;

(C) online contact information collected from a child that is used only to respond more than once directly to a specific request from the child and is not used to recontact the child beyond the scope of that request—

(i) if, before any additional response after the initial response to the child, the operator uses reasonable efforts to provide a parent notice of the online contact information collected from the child, the purposes for which it is to be used, and an opportunity for the parent to request that the operator make no further use of the information and that it not be maintained in retrievable form; or

(ii) without notice to the parent in such circumstances as the Commission may determine are appropriate, taking into consideration the benefits to the child of access to information and services, and risks to the security and privacy of the child, in regulations promulgated under this subsection;

(D) the name of the child and online contact information (to the extent reasonably necessary to protect the safety of a child participant on the site)—

(i) used only for the purpose of protecting such safety;

(ii) not used to recontact the child or for any other purpose; and

(iii) not disclosed on the site, if the operator uses reasonable efforts to provide a parent notice of the name and online contact information collected from the child, the purposes for which it is to be used, and an opportunity for the parent to request that the operator make no further use of the information and that it not be maintained in retrievable form; or

(E) the collection, use, or dissemination of such information by the operator of such a website or online service necessary—

(i) to protect the security or integrity of its website;

(ii) to take precautions against liability;

(iii) to respond to judicial process; or

(iv) to the extent permitted under other provisions of law, to provide information to law enforcement agencies or for an investigation on a matter related to public safety. 1815

(3) TERMINATION OF SERVICE.—The regulations shall permit the operator of a website or an online service to terminate service provided to a child whose parent has refused, under the regulations prescribed under paragraph (1)(B)(ii), to permit the operator's further use or maintenance in retrievable form, or future online collection, of personal information from that child.

(c) ENFORCEMENT.—Subject to sections 1304 and 1306, a violation of a regulation prescribed under subsection (a) shall be treated as a violation of a rule defining an unfair or deceptive act or practice prescribed under section 18(a)(1)(B) of the Federal Trade Commission Act (15 U. S.C. 57a(a)(1)(B)).

(d) INCONSISTENT STATE LAW.—No State or local government may impose any liability for commercial activities or actions by operators in interstate or foreign commerce in connection with an activity or action described in this title that is inconsistent with the treatment of those activities or actions under this section.

SEC. 1304. SAFE HARBORS.

(a) GUIDELINES.—An operator may satisfy the requirements of regulations issued under section 1303(b) by following a set of self-regulatory guidelines, issued by representatives of the marketing or online industries, or by other persons, approved under subsection (b).

(b) INCENTIVES.—

(1) SELF-REGULATORY INCENTIVES.—In prescribing regulations under section 1303, the Commission shall provide incentives for self-regulation by operators to implement the protections afforded children under the regulatory requirements described in subsection (b) of that section.

(2) DEEMED COMPLIANCE.—Such incentives shall include provisions for ensuring that a person will be deemed to be in compliance with the requirements of the regulations under section 1303 if that person complies with guidelines that, after notice and comment, are approved by the Commission upon making a determination that the guidelines meet the requirements of the regulations issued under section 1303.

(3) EXPEDITED RESPONSE TO REQUESTS.—The Commission shall act upon requests for safe harbor treatment within 180 days of the filing of the request, and shall set forth in writing its conclusions with regard to such requests.

(c) APPEALS.—Final action by the Commission on a request for approval of guidelines, or the failure to act within 180 days on a request for approval of guidelines, submitted under subsection (b) may be appealed to a district court of the United States of appropriate jurisdiction as provided for in section 706 of title 5, United States Code.

SEC. 1305. ACTIONS BY STATES.

(a) IN GENERAL.—

(1) CIVIL ACTIONS.—In any case in which the attorney general of a State has reason to believe that an interest of the residents of that State has been or is threatened or adversely affected by the engagement of any person in a practice that violates any regulation of the Commission prescribed under section 1303(b), the State, as parens patriae, may bring a civil action on behalf of the residents of the

State in a district court of the United States of appropriate jurisdiction to—

(A) enjoin that practice;

(B) enforce compliance with the regulation;

(C) obtain damage, restitution, or other compensation on behalf of residents of the State; or

(D) obtain such other relief as the court may consider to be appropriate.

(2) NOTICE.—

(A) IN GENERAL.—Before filing an action under paragraph (1), the attorney general of the State involved shall provide to the Commission—

(i) written notice of that action; and

(ii) a copy of the complaint for that action.

(B) EXEMPTION.—

(i) IN GENERAL.—Subparagraph (A) shall not apply with respect to the filing of an action by an attorney general of a State under this subsection, if the attorney general determines that it is not feasible to provide the notice described in that subparagraph before the filing of the action.

(ii) NOTIFICATION.—In an action described in clause (i), the attorney general of a State shall provide notice and a copy of the complaint to the Commission at the same time as the attorney general files the action.

(b) INTERVENTION.—

(1) IN GENERAL.—On receiving notice under subsection (a)(2), the Commission shall have the right to intervene in the action that is the subject of the notice.

(2) EFFECT OF INTERVENTION.—If the Commission intervenes in an action under subsection (a), it shall have the right—

(A) to be heard with respect to any matter that arises in that action; and

(B) to file a petition for appeal.

(3) AMICUS CURIAE.—Upon application to the court, a person whose self-regulatory guidelines have been approved by the Commission and are relied upon as a defense by any defendant to a proceeding under this section may file amicus curiae in that proceeding.

(c) CONSTRUCTION.—For purposes of bringing any civil action under subsection (a), nothing in this title shall be construed to prevent an attorney general of a State from exercising the powers conferred on the attorney general by the laws of that State to—

(1) conduct investigations;

(2) administer oaths or affirmations; or

(3) compel the attendance of witnesses or the production of documentary and other evidence.

(d) ACTIONS BY THE COMMISSION.—In any case in which an action is instituted by or on behalf of the Commission for violation of any regulation prescribed under section 1303, no State may, during the pendency of that action, institute an action under subsection (a) against any defendant named in the complaint in that action for violation of that regulation.

(e) VENUE; SERVICE OF PROCESS.—

(1) VENUE.—Any action brought under subsection (a) may be brought in the district court of the United States that meets applicable requirements relating to venue under section 1391 of title 28, United States Code.

(2) SERVICE OF PROCESS.—In an action brought under subsection (a), process may be served in any district in which the defendant—

(A) is an inhabitant; or

(B) may be found.

SEC. 1306. ADMINISTRATION AND APPLICABILITY OF ACT.

(a) IN GENERAL.—Except as otherwise provided, this title shall be enforced by the Commission under the Federal Trade Commission Act (15 U.S.C. 41 et seq.).

(b) PROVISIONS.—Compliance with the requirements imposed under this title shall be enforced under—

(1) section 8 of the Federal Deposit Insurance Act (12 U.S.C. 1818), in the case of—

(A) national banks, and Federal branches and Federal agencies of foreign banks, by the Office of the Comptroller of the Currency;

(B) member banks of the Federal Reserve System (other than national banks), branches and agencies of foreign banks (other than Federal branches, Federal agencies, and insured State branches of foreign banks), commercial lending companies owned or controlled by foreign banks, and organizations operating under section 25 or 25(a) of the Federal Reserve Act (12 U.S.C. 601 et seq. and 611 et seq.), by the Board; and

(C) banks insured by the Federal Deposit Insurance Corporation (other than members of the Federal Reserve System) and insured State branches of foreign banks, by the Board of Directors of the Federal Deposit Insurance Corporation;

(2) section 8 of the Federal Deposit Insurance Act (12 U.S.C. 1818), by the Director of the Office of Thrift Supervision, in the case of a savings association the deposits of which are insured by the Federal Deposit Insurance Corporation;

(3) the Federal Credit Union Act (12 U.S.C. 1751 et seq.) by the National Credit Union Administration Board with respect to any Federal credit union;

(4) part A of subtitle VII of title 49, United States Code, by the Secretary of Transportation with respect to any air carrier or foreign air carrier subject to that part;

(5) the Packers and Stockyards Act, 1921 (7 U.S.C. 181 et seq.) (except as provided in section 406 of that Act (7 U.S.C. 226, 227)), by the Secretary of Agriculture with respect to any activities subject to that Act; and

(6) the Farm Credit Act of 1971 (12 U.S.C. 2001 et seq.) by the Farm Credit Administration with respect to any Federal land bank, Federal land bank association, Federal intermediate credit bank, or production credit association.

(c) EXERCISE OF CERTAIN POWERS.—For the purpose of the exercise by any agency referred to in subsection (a) of its powers under any Act referred to in that subsection, a violation of any requirement imposed under this title shall be deemed to be a violation of a requirement imposed under that Act. In addition to its powers under any provision of law specifically referred to in subsection (a), each of the agencies referred to in that subsection may exercise, for the purpose of enforcing compliance with any requirement imposed under this title, any other authority conferred on it by law.

(d) ACTIONS BY THE COMMISSION.—The Commission shall prevent any person from violating a rule of the Commission under section 1303 in the same manner, by the same means, and with the same jurisdiction, powers, and duties as though all applicable terms and provisions of the Federal Trade Commission Act (15 U.S.C. 41 et seq.) were incorporated into and made a part of this title. Any entity that violates such rule shall be subject to the penalties and entitled to the privileges and immunities provided in the Federal Trade Commission Act in the same manner, by the same means, and with the same jurisdiction, power, and duties as though all applicable terms and provisions of the Federal Trade Commission Act were incorporated into and made a part of this title.

(e) EFFECT ON OTHER LAWS.—Nothing contained in the Act shall be construed to limit the authority of the Commission under any other provisions of law.

SEC. 1307. REVIEW.

Not later than 5 years after the effective date of the regulations initially issued under section 1303, the Commission shall—

(1) review the implementation of this title, including the effect of the implementation of this title on practices relating to the collection and disclosure of information relating to children, children's ability to obtain access to information of their choice online, and on the availability of websites directed to children; and

(2) prepare and submit to Congress a report on the results of the review under paragraph (1).

SEC. 1308. EFFECTIVE DATE.

Sections 1303(a), 1305, and 1306 of this title take effect on the later of—

(1) the date that is 18 months after the date of enactment of this Act; or

(2) the date on which the Commission rules on the first application filed for safe harbor treatment under section 1304 if the Commission does not rule on the first such application within one year after the date of enactment of this Act, but in no case later than the date that is 30 months after the date of enactment of this Act.

APPENDIX 15:
CHILDREN'S INTERNET PROTECTION ACT—SELECTED PROVISIONS [PUB. L. NO. 106-554, 12/21/00]

TITLE 42—CHILDREN'S INTERNET PROTECTION

SEC. 1701. SHORT TITLE

This title may be cited as the "Children's Internet Protection Act."

***

SEC. 1711. LIMITATION ON AVAILABILITY OF CERTAIN FUNDS FOR SCHOOLS.

Title III of the Elementary and Secondary Education Act of 1965 (20 U.S.C. 6801 et seq.) is amended by adding at the end the following:

"PART F—LIMITATION ON AVAILABILITY OF CERTAIN FUNDS FOR SCHOOLS

"SEC. 3601. LIMITATION ON AVAILABILITY OF CERTAIN FUNDS FOR SCHOOLS.

"(a) INTERNET SAFETY.—

"(1) IN GENERAL.—No funds made available under this title to a local educational agency for an elementary or secondary school that does not receive services at discount rates under section 254(h)(5) of the Communications Act of 1934, as added by section 1721 of Children's Internet Protection Act, may be used to purchase computers used to access the Internet, or to pay for direct costs associated with accessing the Internet, for such school unless the school, school board, local educational agency, or other authority with responsibility for administration of such school both—

"(A)(i) has in place a policy of Internet safety for minors that includes the operation of a technology protection measure with respect to any of its computers with Internet access that protects against access through such computers to visual depictions that are—

"(I) obscene;

"(II) child pornography; or

"(III) harmful to minors; and

"(ii) is enforcing the operation of such technology protection measure during any use of such computers by minors; and

"(B)(i) has in place a policy of Internet safety that includes the operation of a technology protection measure with respect to any of its computers with Internet access that protects against access through such computers to visual depictions that are—

"(I) obscene; or

"(II) child pornography; and

"(ii) is enforcing the operation of such technology protection measure during any use of such computers.

"(3) **DISABLING DURING CERTAIN USE.**—An administrator, supervisor, or person authorized by the responsible authority under paragraph (1) may disable the technology protection measure concerned to enable access for bona fide research or other lawful purposes.

SEC. 1712. LIMITATION ON AVAILABILITY OF CERTAIN FUNDS FOR LIBRARIES.

"(f) INTERNET SAFETY.—

"(1) **IN GENERAL.**—No funds made available under this Act for a library described in section 213(2)(A) or (B) that does not receive services at discount rates under section 254(h)(6) of the Communications Act of 1934, as added by section 1721 of this Children's Internet Protection Act, may be used to purchase computers used to access the Internet, or to pay for direct costs associated with accessing the Internet, for such library unless—

"(A) such library—

"(i) has in place a policy of Internet safety for minors that includes the operation of a technology protection measure with respect to any of its computers with Internet access that protects against access through such computers to visual depictions that are—

"(I) obscene;

"(II) child pornography; or

"(III) harmful to minors; and

"(ii) is enforcing the operation of such technology protection measure during any use of such computers by minors; and

"(B) such library-

"(i) has in place a policy of Internet safety that includes the operation of a technology protection measure with respect to any of its computers with Internet access that protects against access through such computers to visual depictions that are—

"(I) obscene; or

"(II) child pornography; and

"(ii) is enforcing the operation of such technology protection measure during any use of such computers.

"(3) **DISABLING DURING CERTAIN USE.**—An administrator, supervisor, or other authority may disable a technology protection measure under paragraph (1) to enable access for bona fide research or other lawful purposes.

***

SEC. 1721. REQUIREMENT FOR SCHOOLS AND LIBRARIES TO ENFORCE INTERNET SAFETY POLICIES WITH TECHNOLOGY PROTECTION MEASURES FOR COMPUTERS WITH INTERNET ACCESS AS CONDITION OF UNIVERSAL SERVICE DISCOUNTS.

"(5) **REQUIREMENTS FOR CERTAIN SCHOOLS WITH COMPUTERS HAVING INTERNET ACCESS.**—

"(A) **INTERNET SAFETY.**—

"(i) **IN GENERAL.**—Except as provided in clause (ii), an elementary or secondary school having computers with Internet access may not receive services at discount rates under paragraph (1)(B) unless the school, school board, local educational agency, or other authority with responsibility for administration of the school-

"(I) submits to the Commission the certifications described in subparagraphs (B) and (C);

"(II) submits to the Commission a certification that an Internet safety policy has been adopted and implemented for the school under subsection (l); and

"(III) ensures the use of such computers in accordance with the certifications.

"(B) **CERTIFICATION WITH RESPECT TO MINORS.**—A certification under this subparagraph is a certification that the school, school board, local educational agency, or other authority with responsibility for administration of the school—

"(i) is enforcing a policy of Internet safety for minors that includes monitoring the online activities of minors and the operation of a technology protection measure with respect to any of its computers with Internet access that protects against access through such computers to visual depictions that are—

"(I) obscene;

"(II) child pornography; or

"(III) harmful to minors; and

"(ii) is enforcing the operation of such technology protection measure during any use of such computers by minors.

"(6) **REQUIREMENTS FOR CERTAIN LIBRARIES WITH COMPUTERS HAVING INTERNET ACCESS.**—

'(A) **INTERNET SAFETY.**—

"(i) **IN GENERAL.**—Except as provided in clause (ii), a library having one or more computers with Internet access may not receive services at discount rates under paragraph (1)(B) unless the library—

"(I) submits to the Commission the certifications described in subparagraphs (B) and (C); and

"(II) submits to the Commission a certification that an Internet safety policy has been adopted and implemented for the library under subsection (l); and

"(III) ensures the use of such computers in accordance with the certifications.

"(B) **CERTIFICATION WITH RESPECT TO MINORS.**—A certification under this subparagraph is a certification that the library—

"(i) is enforcing a policy of Internet safety that includes the operation of a technology protection measure with respect to any of its computers with Internet access that protects against access through such computers to visual depictions that are—

"(I) obscene;

"(II) child pornography; or

"(III) harmful to minors; and

"(ii) is enforcing the operation of such technology protection measure during any use of such computers by minors.

***

SEC. 1731. SHORT TITLE.

This subtitle may be cited as the "Neighborhood Children's Internet Protection Act."

SEC. 1732. INTERNET SAFETY POLICY REQUIRED.

Section 254 of the Communications Act of 1934 (47 U.S.C. 254) is amended by adding at the end the following:

"(l) INTERNET SAFETY POLICY REQUIREMENT FOR SCHOOLS AND LIBRARIES.—

"(1) IN GENERAL.—In carrying out its responsibilities under subsection (h), each school or library to which subsection (h) applies shall—

"(A) adopt and implement an Internet safety policy that addresses—

"(i) access by minors to inappropriate matter on the Internet and World Wide Web;

"(ii) the safety and security of minors when using electronic mail, chat rooms, and other forms of direct electronic communications;

"(iii) unauthorized access, including so-called 'hacking,' and other unlawful activities by minors online;

"(iv) unauthorized disclosure, use, and dissemination of personal identification information regarding minors; and

"(v) measures designed to restrict minors' access to materials harmful to minors; and

"(B) provide reasonable public notice and hold at least one public hearing or meeting to address the proposed Internet safety policy.

GLOSSARY

Ad Blocker—Software placed on a user's personal computer that prevents advertisements from being displayed on the Web.

Ad Network—Companies that purchase and place banner advertisements on behalf of their clients.

Affirmative Customization—Refers to a site's or an Internet service provider's use of personal data to tailor or modify the content or design of the site to specifications affirmatively selected by a particular individual.

Aggregate Information—Information that is related to a website visitor but is not about that individual personally, e.g., information kept about which pages on a website are most popular to a visitor but which cannot be traced to the individual personally.

American Civil Liberties Union (ACLU)—A nationwide organization dedicated to the enforcement and preservation of rights and civil liberties guaranteed by the federal and state constitutions.

Anonymity—A situation in which the user's true identity is not known.

Anonymizer—A service that prevents websites from seeing a user's Internet Protocol (IP) address. The service operates as an intermediary to protect the user's identity.

Anonymous Remailer—A special e-mail server that acts as a middleman and strips outgoing e-mail of all personally identifying information, then forwards it to its destination, usually with the IP address of the remailer attached.

Arrest—To deprive a person of his liberty by legal authority.

Authenticate—Process of verifying that the person attempting to send a message or access data is who he or she claims to be.

Authorize—To grant or deny a person access to data or systems.

Avatar—Graphical representation of a user in a virtual world set in cyberspace.

Banner Ad—Advertisement for a product or company that is placed on a web page in order to sell site visitors a good or service. Clicking on a banner will take the visitor to a site to learn more about that product or service.

Bill of Rights—The first eight amendments to the United States Constitution.

Blocking Software—A computer program that allows parents, teachers, or guardians to "block" access to certain websites and other information available over the Internet.

Bookmark—A bookmark is an online function that lets the user access their favorite websites quickly.

Browser—A browser is special software that allows the user to navigate several areas of the Internet and view a website.

Bulletin Board Systems—Electronic networks of computers that are connected by a central computer setup and operated by a system administrator or operator and are distinguishable from the Internet by their "dial-up" accessibility. BBS users link their individual computers to the central BBS computer by a modem that allows them to post messages, read messages left by others, trade information, or hold direct conversations. Access to a BBS can, and often is, privileged and limited to those users who have access privileges granted by the systems operator.

Burden of Proof—The duty of a party to substantiate an allegation or issue to convince the trier of fact as to the truth of their claim.

Cache—A place on the computer's hard drive where the browser stores information from pages or sites that the user has visited so that returning to those pages or sites is faster and easier.

Capacity—Capacity is the legal qualification concerning the ability of one to understand the nature and effects of one's acts.

Chat Room—A chat room is a place for people to converse online by typing messages to each other. A number of customers can be in the public chat rooms at any given time, which are monitored for illegal activity and even appropriate language by systems operators (SYSOP). The public chat rooms usually cover a broad range of topics such as entertainment, sports, game rooms, children only, etc.

Chat—Real-time text conversation between users in a chat room with no expectation of privacy. All chat conversation is accessible by all individuals in the chat room while the conversation is taking place.

Chief Justice—The presiding member of certain courts, which have more than one judge, e.g., the United States Supreme Court.

CIPA—Children's Internet Protection Act of 2000.

Ciphertext—Scrambled, unreadable contents of an encrypted message or file.

Circuit—A judicial division of a state or the United States.

Circuit Court—One of several courts in a given jurisdiction.

Citation—A reference to a source of legal authority, such as a case or statute.

Civil Disobedience—The refusal to obey a law for the purpose of demonstrating its unfairness.

Common Law—Common law is the system of jurisprudence that originated in England and was later applied in the United States. The common law is based on judicial precedent rather than statutory law.

Conclusion of Fact—A conclusion reached by natural inference and based solely on the facts presented.

Conclusion of Law—A conclusion reached through the application of rules of law.

Conclusive Evidence—Evidence that is incontrovertible.

Consent—Explicit permission, given to a website by a visitor, to handle personal information in specified ways. "Informed consent" implies that the company fully discloses its information practices prior to obtaining personal data or permission to use it.

Constitution—The fundamental principles of law that frame a governmental system.

Constitutional Right—Refers to the individual liberties granted by the constitution of a state or the federal government.

Cookie—When the user visits a site, a notation may be fed to a file known as a "cookie" in their computer for future reference. If the user revisits the site, the "cookie" file allows the website to identify the user as a "return" guest and offers the user products tailored to their interests or tastes.

Cookie Buster—Software that is designed to block the placement of cookies by ad networks and websites thus preventing companies from tracking a user's activity.

COPA—Child Online Protection Act of 1998.

Court—The branch of government responsible for the resolution of disputes arising under the laws of the government.

Criminal Impersonation—As it pertains to identity theft, means to knowingly assume a false or fictitious identity or capacity, and in that identity or capacity, doing any act with intent to unlawfully gain a benefit or injure or defraud another.

Culpable—Referring to conduct, it is that which is deserving of moral blame.

Cyberspace—Cyberspace is another name for the Internet.

Data Spill—The result of a poorly designed form on a website which may cause an information leak to web servers of other companies, such as an ad network or advertising agency.

Decrypt—To decode data from its protected, scrambled form so it can be read.

Defamation—The publication of an injurious statement about the reputation of another.

Defendant—In a civil proceeding, the party responding to the complaint.

Defense—Opposition to the truth or validity of the plaintiff's claims.

Digital Certificate—Process using encryption technology whereby a document can be digitally stamped or certified as to its place of origin, and a certification authority supports and legitimizes the certificates.

Digital Signature—A digital signature is a digital certification or stamp that uses encryption technology to authenticate an individual's signature is legitimate.

Digital storm—Analytic tools currently being developed by the FBI to sift and link data from disparate sources.

Directories—Indexes of web pages organized by subject.

District Attorney—An officer of a governmental body with the duty to prosecute those accused of crimes.

Download—A download is the transfer of files or software from a remote computer to the user's computer.

Downstream Data Use—Refers to companies' practice of disclosing personal information collected from users to other parties downstream to facilitate a transaction.

Dynamic IP Address—An IP address that changes every time a user logs on, or dials-up, to a computer.

Encryption—The scrambling of digital information so that it is unreadable to the average user. A computer must have "digital keys" to unscramble and read the information.

Encryption Software—Often used as a security measure, encryption software scrambles data so that it is unreadable to interceptors without the appropriate information to read the data.

E-mail—E-mail is computer-to-computer messages between one or more individuals via the Internet.

Ethernet—A commonly used networking technology that links computers together.

Ethernet Adapter Address—The personal name of the Ethernet card in a user's computer.

Extended Service Set Identifier (ESSID)—The name a manufacturer assigns to a router. It may be a standard, default name assigned by the manufacturer to all hardware of that model. Users can improve security by changing to a unique name.

Felony—A crime of a graver or more serious nature than those designated as misdemeanors.

File Transfer Protocol (FTP)—A way to transfer files from one computer to another.

Filter—Filter is software the user can buy that lets the user block access to websites and content that they may find unsuitable.

Fine—A financial penalty imposed upon a defendant.

Firewall—Hardware or software designed to keep hackers from using another's computer to send personal information without the owner's permission. Firewalls watch for outside attempts to access the system and blocks communications to and from unauthorized sources.

First Amendment—The First Amendment of the United States Constitution protects the right to freedom of religion and freedom of expression from government interference.

Fraud—Fraud is a false representation of a matter of fact, whether by words or by conduct, by false or misleading allegations, or by concealment of that which should have been disclosed, which deceives and is intended to deceive another so that he shall act upon it to his legal injury.

Globally Unique Identifier (GUID)—A unique code used to identify a computer, user, file, etc., for tracking purposes.

Hardware—The computer and related machines such as scanners and printers.

Harmful to Minors—A term used to describe any picture, image, graphic image file, or other visual depiction that: (a) taken as a whole and with respect to minors, appeals to a prurient interest in nudity, sex, or excretion; (b) depicts, describes, or represents, in a patently offensive way with respect to what is suitable for minors, an actual or simulated sexual act or sexual contact, actual or simulated normal or perverted sexual acts, or a lewd exhibition of the genitals; and (c) taken as a whole, lacks serious literary, artistic, political, or scientific value as to minors.

Host Name—Each computer is given a name, which typically includes the user name and the organizational owner of the computer.

Home Page—The first page or document web users see when connecting to a web server or when visiting a website.

Hyperlink—An image or portion of text on a web page that is linked to another web page. The user clicks on the link to go to another web page or another place on the same page.

Hypertext Markup Language (HTML)—The standard language used for creating documents on the Internet.

Hypertext Transfer Protocol (HTTP)—The standard language that computers connected to the Internet use to communicate with each other.

Ignorance—Lack of knowledge.

Ignorantia Legis Non Excusat—Latin for "Ignorance of the law is no excuse." Although an individual may not think an act is illegal, the act is still punishable.

Illegal—Against the law.

Injunction—A judicial remedy either requiring a party to perform an act, or restricting a party from continuing a particular act.

Instant message (IP)—A chat-like technology on an online service that notifies a user when another person is online, allowing for simultaneous communication.

Internet—The Internet is the universal network that allows computers to talk to other computers in words, text, graphics, and sound, anywhere in the world.

Internet Access Service—A service that enables users to access content, information, electronic mail, or other services offered over the Internet, and may also include access to proprietary content, information, and other services as part of a package of services offered to consumers.

Internet Information Location tool—A service that refers or links users to an online location on the World Wide Web. Such term includes directories, indices, references, pointers, and hypertext links.

Internal Protocol (IP)—The standards by which computers talk to each other over the Internet.

Internet Service Provider (ISP)—A service that allows the user to connect to the Internet.

IP Address—A number or series of numbers that identify a computer linked to the Internet and which is generally written as four numbers separated by periods, e.g., 12.24.36.48.

JavaScript—A programming language used to add features to web pages in order to make the website more interactive.

Junk E-mail—Unsolicited commercial e-mail also known as "spam."

Keyword—A word the user enters into a search engine to begin the search for specific information or websites.

Liability—Liability refers to one's obligation to do or refrain from doing something, such as the payment of a debt.

Libel—A form of unprotected speech involving the false and malicious publication of defamatory words that are written or broadcast.

Links—Links are highlighted words on a website that allow the user to connect to other parts of the same website or to other websites.

Listserve—Listserve is an online mailing list that allows individuals or organizations to send e-mail to groups of people at one time.

Local Area Network (LAN)—A computer network limited to the immediate area, usually the same building or floor of a building.

Media Access Control (MAC) Address—A unique number that the manufacturer assigns to each computer or other device in a network.

Minor—A person who has not yet reached the age of legal competence, which is designated as 18 in most states.

Misdemeanor—Criminal offenses that are less serious than felonies and carry lesser penalties.

Modem—A modem is an internal or external device that connects the computer to a phone line and, if the user wishes, to a company that can link the user to the Internet.

Mouse—A small device attached to the computer by a cord, which lets the user give commands to the computer by clicking.

Offense—Any misdemeanor or felony violation of the law for which a penalty is prescribed.

Online Profiling—The practice of aggregating information about consumers' preferences and interests, gathered primarily by tracking their online movements and actions, with the purpose of creating targeted advertisement using the resulting profiles.

Online Service—An online service is an ISP with added information, entertainment and shopping features.

Operating System—The main program that runs on a computer.

Operator—The person who is responsible for maintaining and running a website.

Opinion—The reasoning behind a court's decision.

Opt-In—Refers to when a user gives explicit permission for a company to use personal information for marketing purposes.

Opt-Out—Refers to when a user prohibits a company from using personal information for marketing purposes.

Original Jurisdiction—The jurisdiction of a court to hear a matter in the first instance.

Overrule—A holding in a particular case is overruled when the same court, or a higher court, in that jurisdiction, makes an opposite ruling in a subsequent case on the identical point of law ruled upon in the prior case.

Packet—Term for the small bundles of digital information passed between users and sites.

Packet Sniffer—A software tool used to track the packets of information sent to and from a computer.

Password—A password is a personal code that the user selects to access their account with their ISP.

Personally Identifiable Information (PII)—Refers to information such as name, mailing address, phone number, or e-mail address.

Phishing—The term "phishing" refers to a type of deception designed to steal a computer user's valuable personal data, such as credit card numbers, passwords, account data, social security number, financial records, or other information. Phishing is typically carried out using e-mail. The e-mail appears to be coming from a trusted website.

Ping—A short message sent by a computer across a network to another computer confirming that the target computer is up and running.

Platform for Privacy Preferences Project (P3P)—A proposed browser feature that would analyze privacy policies and allow a user to control what personal information is revealed to a particular site.

Precedent—A previously decided case that is recognized as authority for the disposition of future cases.

Preference Data—Data, which may be collected by a site or a service provider about an individual's likes and dislikes.

Pretexting—The practice of fraudulently obtaining personal financial information, such as account numbers and balances, by calling financial institutions under the pretext of being a customer.

Pretty Good Privacy (PGP)—A widely used encryption software.

Private Key—A data file assigned to a single individual to use in decrypting messages previously encrypted through use of that person's key.

Privacy Policy—A statement on a website describing what information about the user is collected by the site and how it is used; also known as a privacy statement or privacy notice.

Privacy Seal Program—A program that certifies a site's compliance with the standards of privacy protection. Only those sites that comply with the standards are able to note certification.

Proxy Server—A proxy server is a system that caches items from other servers to speed up access.

Pseudonymity—A situation in which the user has taken on an assumed identity.

Public Defender—A lawyer hired by the government to represent an indigent person accused of a crime.

Public Forum—Refers to a digital entity such as a bulletin board, public directory, or commercial CD-ROM directory, where personal user data may be distributed by a site or a service provider.

Public Key—A data file assigned to a specific person but which others can use to send the person encrypted messages. Because public keys don't contain the components necessary to decrypt messages, they are safe to distribute to others.

Query String—The extended string of a URL after the standard website address.

Rational Basis Test—The constitutional analysis of a law to determine whether it has a reasonable relationship to some legitimate government objective so as to uphold the law.

Router—A device that connects two or more networks. A router finds the best path for forwarding information across the networks.

Sanction—A form of punishment.

Screen Name—The name the user selects to be known by when the user communicates online.

Search Engine—A function that lets the user search for information and websites. Search engines or search functions may be found on many websites.

Search Warrant—A judicial order authorizing and directing law enforcement officials to search a specified location for specific items or individuals.

Secondary Use—Refers to using personal information collected for one purpose for a second, unrelated purpose.

Secure Anonymous Remailer—Websites that will strip a consumer's identifying information so they can surf other websites and send e-mail anonymously.

Server—A host computer that stores information and/or software programs and makes them available to users of other computers.

Slander—Spoken words that are damaging to the reputation of another.

Spam—E-mail from a company or charity that is unsolicited and sent to many people at one time, usually for advertising purposes; also known as junk e-mail.

Static IP Address—An IP address that remains the same each time a user logs on or dials up a server.

Supreme Court—In most jurisdictions, the Supreme Court is the highest appellate court, including the federal court system.

Testify—The offering of a statement in a judicial proceeding, under oath and subject to the penalty of perjury.

Testimony—The sworn statement made by a witness in a judicial proceeding.

Third Party Ad Server—Companies that put banner advertising on websites that are generally not owned by that advertiser.

Third Party Cookie—A cookie that is placed by a party other than the user or the website being viewed, such as advertising or marketing groups who are trying to gather data on general consumer use.

Trace Route—The course that a packet travels across the Internet from one computer to another.

Tracker GIF—Electronic images, usually not visible to site visitors, that allow a website to count those who have visited that page or to access certain cookies; also known as a "Clear GIF."

Trial—The judicial procedure whereby disputes are determined based on the presentation of issues of law and fact. Issues of fact are decided by the trier of fact, either the judge or jury, and issues of law are decided by the judge.

Trial Court—The court of original jurisdiction over a particular matter.

TRUSTe—An online privacy seal program that certifies eligible websites, holding sites to baseline privacy standards. TRUSTe requires its licensees to implement certain fair information practices and to submit to various types of compliance monitoring in order to display a privacy seal on their websites.

Trustmark—An online seal awarded by TRUSTe to websites that agree to post their privacy practices openly via privacy statements, as well as adhere to enforcement procedures that ensure that those privacy promises are met.

Unconstitutional—Refers to a statute which conflicts with the United States Constitution, rendering it void.

Undue Influence—The exertion of improper influence upon another for the purpose of destroying that person's free will in carrying out a particular act.

Uniform Resource Locator (URL)—The address that lets the user locate a particular site. For example, http://www.ftc.gov is the URL for the Federal Trade Commission. Government URLs end in ".gov" and non-profit organizations and trade associations end in ".org." Commercial companies generally end in ".com," although additional suffixes or domains may be used as the number of Internet businesses grows.

Unique Identifiers—Non-financial identifiers issued for purposes of consistently identifying the individual.

Upload—Copying or sending data or documents from one computer to another computer.

Use—Refers to the practice of collecting and using personal data internally, within the company or organization, for both administrative and marketing purposes.

User—An individual on whose behalf a service is accessed and for which personal data exists.

V-Chip—A microchip installed in television sets for the specific purpose of allow parents to screen out undesirable programming.

Verdict—The definitive answer given by the jury to the court concerning the matters of fact committed to the jury for their deliberation and determination.

Verifiable Parental Consent—A type of parental consent obtained by a website to collect information from children under age 13 which must be verifiable, e.g., by written permission or a credit card number.

Virus—A virus is a file maliciously planted in the user's computer that can damage files and disrupt their system.

Void—Having no legal force or binding effect.

Web Bug—A graphic in a website or enhanced e-mail message that enables a third party to monitor who is reading the page or message.

Website—A website is an Internet destination where the user can look at and retrieve data. All the websites in the world, linked together, make up the World Wide Web or the "Web."

Wired Equivalent Privacy (WEP)—A security protocol that encrypts data sent to and from wireless devices within a network. Not as strong as WPA encryption.

Wi-Fi Protected Access (WPA)—A security protocol developed to fix flaws in WEP. Encrypts data sent to and from wireless devices within a network.

Wireless Network—A method of connecting a computer to other computers or to the Internet without linking them by cables.

BIBLIOGRAPHY AND ADDITIONAL RESOURCES

American Express Company (Date Visited: October 2008) http://www.americanexpress.com/

Better Business Bureau On-Line (Date Visited: October 2008) http://www.bbbonline.org/

Black's Law Dictionary, Fifth Edition. St. Paul, MN: West Publishing Company, 1979.

Center for Democracy and Technology (Date Visited: October 2008) http://www.consumerprivacyguide.org/

Consumer Sentinel Network (Date Visited: October 2008) http://www.ftc.gov/sentinel/

CyberAngels (Date Visited: October 2008) http://www.cyberangels.org/

Direct Marketing Association (Date Visited: October 2008) http://www.the-dma.org/

Federal Bureau of Investigation Internet Crime Complaint Center (Date Visited: October 2008) http://www.fbi.gov/

Federal Citizen Information Center (Date Visited: October 2008) http://www.pueblo.gsa.gov/

Federal Deposit Insurance Corporation (Date Visited: October 2008) http://www.fdic.gov/

Federal Trade Commission (Date Visited: October 2008) http://www.ftc.gov/

Get Net Wise (Date Visited: October 2008) http://www.getnetwise.org/

Identity Theft Resource Center (Date Visited: October 2008) http://www.idtheftcenter.org/

Internet Alliance (Date Visited: October 2008) http://www.internetalliance.org/

National Center for Missing and Exploited Children (Date Visited: October 2008) http://www.missingkids.com/

National Consumer's League (Date Visited: October 2008) http://natlconsumersleague.org/

Online Privacy Alliance (Date Visited: October 2008) http://www.privacyalliance.org/

PEW Internet and American Life Project (Date Visited: October 2008) http://www.pewinternet.org/

Privacy Rights Clearinghouse (Date Visited: October 2008) http://www.privacyrights.org/

Truste (Date Visited: October 2008) http://www.truste.org/

United States Department of Justice (Date Visited: October 2008) http://www.usdoj.gov/criminal/fraud/websites/idtheft.html/

United States Department of Justice Computer Crime & Intellectual Property Section (Date Visited: October 2008) http://www.usdoj.gov/criminal/cybercrime/ccpolicy.html/

United States General Accounting Office (Date Visited: October 2008) http://www.gao.gov/

United States Office of the Attorney General (Date Visited: October 2008) http://www.usdoj.gov/ag/

United States Secret Service (Date Visited: October 2008) http://www.treas.gov/usss/

United States Social Security Administration (Date Visited: October 2008) http://www.ssa.gov/

Whois.Net (Date Visited: October 2008) http://www.whois.net/

Wired Kids (Date Visited: October 2008) http://www.wiredkids.org/